ABOUT THE AUTHOR

Laura Vanderkam is the best-selling author of *What the Most Successful People Do Before Breakfast, All the Money in the World, 168 Hours, Grindhopping* and *I Know How She Does It*. She is the co-host, with Sarah Hart-Unger, of the podcast Best of Both Worlds. Her TED talk, 'How to gain control of your free time', has been viewed more than 5 million times. Her work has appeared in *The Wall Street Journal, The New York Times, Fortune* and other publications. She lives with her husband and their four children outside Philadelphia.

Lauravanderkam.com

OFF THE CLOCK

CLCK

FEEL LESS BUSY
WHILE GETTING MORE DONE

LAURA VANDERKAM

piatkus

PIATKUS

First published in the US in 2018 by Portfolio, an imprint of
Penguin Random House LLC
First published in Great Britain in 2018 by Piatkus

1 3 5 7 9 10 8 6 4 2

A CIP catalogue record for this book
is available from the British Library.

ISBN 978-0-349-42117-9

Printed and bound in Great Britain by
Clays Ltd, St Ives plc

Papers used by Piatkus are from well-managed forests
and other responsible sources.

MIX
Paper from
responsible sources
FSC
www.fsc.org
FSC® C104740

To Alex

In science that day, Dr. Pavlica had mentioned the speed of light, and I'd heard 'the speed of *life*.' While he was going on about $E = mc^2$, I was thinking again about how crazy it is that life just speeds along, sunrise after sunrise, season after season. Whether you're totally miserable or insanely happy, the months keep coming, crashing like waves. There are no do-overs, no backsies, and bad stuff happens. But then I thought, *Wait. Good stuff happens too. And sometimes, even a kiss can slow time down.*

—Carol Weston, *Speed of Life*

CONTENTS

OFF THE CL⏰CK

OFF THE CLOCK

THE TIME PARADOX

I look upon time as no more than an idea.

—Mary Oliver, "When Death Comes"

One July Friday not long ago, I woke in a hotel room in the little town of Bar Harbor, Maine. My husband, Michael, and I had originally planned to go on a work trip for him that weekend, and so my mother and aunt had come to watch our four small children. Then we found out he didn't have to go. We seized the opportunity to take a grown-ups-only hiking trip in Acadia National Park. I took the last flight from Philadelphia on Thursday night, and drove through a midnight storm from Bangor to the coast. Michael, coming from Seattle, planned to meet me there around lunch the next day.

So on Friday morning, I was by myself. I drifted awake, put on my running clothes, and took off to explore. It was a gorgeous summer morning. The newly risen sun had washed away all traces of rain and fog from the night before. I ran in the direction of the ocean, and entered the town proper as Bar Harbor was waking up. Breakfast smells drifted out of the restaurants. Just as in Robert McCloskey's children's book *One Morning in Maine,* I saw boats, evergreens, the hills. A light wind blew off the waves. This mist made the July heat gentle on my bare arms. It was so pleasant as I pounded along the narrow path by the water, full of rocks and flowers, that I was thinking of little until the usual sensation popped into my head: *OK, what time is it? What do I have to do next?*

But there was no required next thing. I was free to do what I wished. I recalled a phrase from the summer when I was seventeen and taking dinner orders at Fazoli's restaurant on Indiana's State Route 933. Come the end of my shift, I would punch out to a liberated state: I was off the clock.

That sense of time freedom is magical. It is also, for many of us, a rare and fleeting feeling. Though my work has become shockingly cushier since that $4.90/hour summer, other obligations—such as those I was fleeing in Maine—have conspired to create a reality where I can name the few days in recent years when I have felt this total freedom. As I wrote in my journal of one such day I'd managed to create on a trip to San Diego:

> *I can't say I had any particularly deep thoughts . . . Just a lot of staring at the ocean and reading and thinking. And walking 20,000 steps. It was nice to feel unhurried. No clock ticking in the background, no one waiting for me, so I could watch the sunset in peace. All of it. I think that has been the*

aspect of having kids that is the hardest—being constantly accountable for my time.

Any busy person can sympathize with that feeling, and I suppose my life falls into this category. My husband and I both have careers that involve clients and travel. Our children—Jasper, Sam, Ruth, and Alex—are, as I write this, all age ten and under. With all the moving parts, it makes sense that I would need to know where the time goes, but because I make my living speaking and writing about time management, which makes a virtue of accountability, I must grapple with my mixed emotions more intensely than most.

Feeling off the clock is exhilarating. It is a key component of human happiness. And yet a life is lived in hours, and living the good life requires being a proper steward of those hours. This stewardship often requires choices that come from being mindful of time. My free morning in Maine required figuring out the logistics of childcare, flights, and car rentals. Being off the clock in San Diego demanded similar logistics. It also meant bringing myself to that transcendent ocean rather than scrolling through social media posts on other people's transcendent ocean experiences. More broadly, it is hard to relax and enjoy time when there are looming projects whose constituent parts have not been mapped out, or amid the malaise of knowing swaths of your "wild and precious life," as the poet Mary Oliver puts it, are lost to the vague anxiety of traffic, aimless meetings, and such that the brain doesn't even catalog in memory.

So we come to some paradoxes. Being off the clock implies time freedom, yet time freedom stems from time discipline. You must know where the time goes in order to transcend the ceaseless ticking.

You can wander into philosophical knots on such matters, knots you might need to run miles along the coast to sort out, but I believe that part of wisdom is knowing that two contradictory concepts can both be right when seen from a broader perspective. The key is finding the right vantage point on the cliff to take in the full view.

This book is about finding that lookout spot for understanding time freedom. It is about developing a new mind-set. There will always be tension between knowing how we spend our time and moving beyond an obsession with the minutes. Yet this tension does not mean that both aren't simultaneously possible. Honoring time requires embracing certain truths: that time is precious *and* time is plentiful. Time is finite, so we must make smart choices about it. But time is also abundant: there is enough for anything that truly matters.

Who Feels Pressed for Time?

Much discussion of modern life is premised on the first part of this paradox. Colleagues answer the "How was your weekend?" greeting on Monday morning with the ubiquitous "Busy." Trend stories assume we are all starved for time, though a closer look at this perception finds that "all" is stretching things. During a recent trip to the gym on a Saturday morning—fit in after dropping off Sam at a wrestling meet for his team warm-up, but before his first match—I noted that the older ladies who'd just exited the pool and were in the locker room with me were *still in there* after I came back from running three miles on the treadmill. Why not? They were enjoying one another's company. There was no rush.

Gallup conducts frequent polls on time stress. In 2015, the organization found that people who are employed are far more likely to say they do not have the time to do the things they want to do (61 percent) than people, such as retirees, who are not working (32 percent). Likewise, people with children at home are more likely to report that they feel this time stress (61 percent) than people without kids at home (42 percent).

These statistics imply that the secret of time abundance is simple: stop working and skip having a family. The problem is that these choices present obvious drawbacks. Plus, it oversimplifies the equation. If six in ten people who are employed, or have children, feel pressed for time, that means four in ten people with similar responsibilities do have time for things they want to do.

In years of studying schedules, I've met plenty of seemingly busy people in this latter camp. Despite almost infinite demands on their time, they seem . . . *relaxed*. I well recall a conversation with an executive I hoped to interview about her astonishing productivity. I began our call with an assurance that I would not take much of her time. She laughed. "Oh, I have all the time in the world," she said.

This wasn't technically true, but what she meant is that she had chosen to talk with me, and she had structured her life so that other things would wait while she focused on what she deemed worthy. She didn't have to rush. Whatever I was racing off to, she was off the clock. To be sure, she had the support system to allow this, including an assistant who could manage interruptions. As I have met more people like her, though, I've realized that often their serenity doesn't stem from the fact that they can make other people wait for them. There isn't much crowding on their calendars when they don't want things on their calendars.

This same mind-set is reflected in people we have all encountered who don't seem to accept the normal limits of what is possible with time. They have blossoming careers. They enjoy their families and friends. They exercise most days, and volunteer, and read those books that the rest of us claim our frenzied lives won't allow time for.

It is an enviable level of calm. It is a mind-set I am curious about. How do busy people who feel relaxed about time structure their lives? What habits do they have? What choices do they make?

A Time-Diary Study

I like hearing people's stories about their schedules, but I like data too. So in early 2017, I set out to answer my questions systematically. I recruited more than nine hundred people, all of whom fell into both of those categories that Gallup found were most associated with time stress: they worked for pay (I specified for thirty-plus hours each week), and they had children under age eighteen living at home.

On March 28, I asked them questions about their lives: their commutes, their exercise habits, what they did before bed on weekdays. Then I had them recount how they had spent the previous day—Monday, March 27, 2017—hour by hour. Finally, I had them answer questions on how they felt about their time on that Monday and how they felt about their time generally. People rated how much they agreed or disagreed with statements of time abundance such as "Generally, I feel like I have enough time for the things I want to do" and "Yesterday, I generally felt present rather than distracted."

Each person got a time-perception score based on their answers to thirteen questions, each of which ran along a seven-point scale from "strongly disagree" (1) to "strongly agree" (7). My research team analyzed the time logs for key words. We looked at the differences between people with high time-perception scores (in the top 20 percent of numerical scores for the survey) and low time-perception scores (in the bottom 20 percent). We also looked more deeply into the time logs of our outliers: those in the top and bottom 3 percent.

The answers were fascinating. Monday, March 27, 2017, contained the same quantity of time for everyone I studied, but feelings about those twenty-four hours diverged widely. Intriguingly, people felt better about their time "yesterday" than they did about their time generally, a phenomenon that supports other time-diary study findings that "yesterday" people worked less, slept more, and had more leisure time than in the picture of their lives they keep in their minds.

Still, the answers on how people spent their time uncovered significant, and occasionally counterintuitive, insights. I think these revelations are important for anyone of any demographic— including those without kids at home but with many other commitments—who wants to feel less busy while getting more done.

First, people who feel like they have enough time are exceedingly mindful of their time. They know where the time goes. They accept ownership of their lives and think through their days and weeks ahead of time. They also reflect on their lives, figuring out what worked and what didn't.

They build adventures into their lives. They do this even on a normal March Monday, knowing that rich memories can expand time both as they are being created and in the rearview mirror.

They scrub their lives of anything that does not belong there. This includes self-imposed time burdens, such as constant connectivity, that clog time for no good reason. Indeed, one of the most striking findings of my survey was the gap in estimated phone checks per hour between people who felt relaxed about time and those who felt anxious.

People who feel like they have enough time know how to

linger in moments that deserve their attention; they can stretch the present when the present is worth being stretched.

They spend their resources to maximize happiness, yet when unpleasantness cannot be avoided, they figure out how to cope with and even savor time that others might wish away.

They let go of expectations of perfection and big results in the short run. Instead, they decide that good enough is good enough, knowing that steady progress over the long run is unstoppable.

Finally, they know that people are a good use of time. I found that people who spent quality time with friends and family on that March Monday were more likely than people who spent that March Monday watching TV to feel like they had enough time for the things they wanted to do.

This book looks at how to build these skills for feeling less busy and getting more done into daily life.

These strategies can help anyone achieve time freedom. They can help if your life feels out of control, but they can also help if you feel like much of your relationship with time works, and you simply want to take your career, your relationships, and your personal happiness to the next level. Despite the usual reputation of self-help, the truth is that most self-help readers already have their lives together. People pick up books on time management because their lives are good, and yet they can see in that goodness that there is space for even more wonder.

Life offers possibilities we have only begun to imagine. The lure is a life that is full and calm. Most of us want to claim more joy from our hours for this simple reason: a life is made of hours, like all those hours recorded from March 27, 2017. How we live those hours—and whether we make the most of those hours—will add up to how we live our lives.

How Few Are Our Days?

This brings us back to the original paradox at the heart of using time well. How can time be precious *and* plentiful? I suspect the knottiness of this question stems from these being positive words. Put a negative twist on them (scarce, tedious) and we arrive at the simple, rued reality of life: we count down time to the next thing, even knowing that time in the grand sense dwindles like sand in an hourglass.

The days are long, but the years are short. We know from the dates surrounding the dash on any biography that life spans are limited. On April 15, 2017, an Italian woman named Emma Morano passed away. Born on November 29, 1899, she was the last living person known to have been born in the 1800s. That century wasn't ancient history. Things that happened then affect life now, but all that is institutional memory. No human now breathing on this planet experienced them.

"Make us know how few are our days, that our minds may learn wisdom," implores the psalmist. I have lately begun the midlife indulgence of calculating those days. Tables from the Centers for Disease Control reveal that a woman like me, born in 1978, could, at birth, expect to live 78.0 years. That gives me 683,760 hours of life, building in leap years. As I write this a bit past my thirty-eighth birthday, I exist on time's pivot point. Close to half is done and gone, leaving me some 350,640 hours. Of course, this at-birth expectancy reflects child and adolescent mortality, which it seems I avoided. Should I make it to age sixty-five, I could expect to expire at 83.4 years, which buys me another 47,328 hours. All told, the odds give me about 400,000 hours of life left to go.

At first glance this seems expansive enough, even if it is give-or-take pretty much the full sum. Dividing it by more recognizable quantities makes it more sobering. An eight-hour span of sleep is 1/50,000th of my expected remaining life. A forty-hour workweek is 1/10,000 of my time. As I'll discuss later, I track my time on weekly spreadsheets; each Monday I open a new one. Should I continue with this habit, I have about 2,381 more weekly spreadsheets left to open. If I live to age 83.4, I have just forty-five more times to see the flowers bloom in the spring, and I will shuffle off this mortal coil precisely as they bloom that forty-fifth time.

Such realizations are what the medieval monks called *memento mori*—moments when we see how few are our days—and yet as I try to place events in relation to the magnolias and plum trees blooming the past few times, it feels like even recent bloomings happened ages ago. Four Aprils before I wrote this I had no idea that my fourth child would come into my life. But now I think, *Was there ever a time before Alex?*

This is the nature of time perception: there is little straightforward about it. A night in the ER seems endless, the second hand on the hospital clock almost ceasing to move. Meanwhile, the country singer implores us "don't blink" lest we miss the decades rushing past.

Time warps as we view longer sections of it. A song on the radio the other day triggered my memories of the spring of 1996. I was seventeen years old. I pondered that the twenty-one years that had passed between then and that moment could be divided into three segments of seven years, marked off by events that define my current life. I met my husband in early 2003. My first book on time management was published in 2010. And yet the years between 1996 and 2003 seem longer in retrospect than those between 2003 and 2010, at least until I look through old calendars and recall what consumed my time. Then those years swell in my reckoning as I recount long trips, or writing books that consumed many hours but that few people read. I recall my pregnancies feeling very long. I marked each week's passing. Then when the children were born, I no longer noted each Thursday going by. Time slowed, then it sped.

If time seems to move at different paces depending on circumstance, this raises intriguing questions: Can we alter our perception of time by interacting with it in different ways? Can we develop the skills necessary to make good times pass as slowly as bad times?

I do think it is possible, at least to a degree. This book is partly about my attempts to make time feel fuller and richer, to make these years that everyone says are so short feel more like an intricate tapestry than a slick linoleum floor. I try to linger on life's pivot point a bit longer. I look for space in this circus of a life. I try to make the most of those 400,000 hours slipping from one side of the hourglass to the other.

Freedom Is Multifaceted

Because life is complex, being off the clock and experiencing time freedom is likewise a complicated concept. This book explores different ways we can interact with and escape time's ceaseless ticking. In some cases, being off the clock can mean the absence of any obligations, like my morning in Maine. This is a lovely way to spend some quantity of time, particularly if you have a lot of what feel like have-to-dos in your life. People who spend their days waking up too early to commute too far to jobs where too many hours are dictated will likely view being off the clock as the traditional definition: not working.

And yet as I study people who feel that time is abundant, I see that it is possible to feel off the clock even while doing paid work. When you are absorbed in solving an interesting problem, you can lose all sense of time, just as might happen during a dinner with old friends. And in arranging that dinner with old friends, we soon see that while we can feel relaxed when we have no time-specific obligations, as I did on that morning in Maine, sometimes having plans can make us feel more relaxed than not having plans. Lingering over wine with friends requires inviting them over, and being mindful of the time that will happen, but then once they are there we enjoy ourselves so much more, and feel so much more like time is abundant, than if we were spending an equivalent evening doing what most people do when they have nothing on the calendar: watching TV or glancing at their phones just often enough to feel on edge.

Sometimes commitments literally give us more time. In one of the most famous experiments in social science, elderly residents of a nursing home given plants to care for lived longer and were in better health than those without such responsibilities. Better health and longevity means you are free to do things you otherwise would not be able to. This phenomenon shows up in other contexts of obligation as well. A strong marriage meets enough emotional needs that people feel free to take big risks in the outside world. Having children takes a ton of work, and yet the emotional intensity of raising them can slow time down, if you open yourself to that possibility.

Perhaps this sounds like another paradox: freedom does not mean having zero obligations, but I think it's helpful to see that freedom is multifaceted. It must be viewed from a broader vantage point to be understood. There is freedom *from* things we don't want to do, but there is also freedom *to* do the things we want to do, and figuring out the right balance requires understanding when commitments are burdens and when they are benefits.

Ultimately, in my definition, time freedom is about having blissful moments of no immediate obligations, like on my Maine morning, and also choosing obligations—including lines cast

into the future in the form of plans—with an eye toward building a life that allows for meaning and a sense of time's abundance.
It is about going full-in on these commitments so they become
sources of identity. Caring about community is abstract, but
tending a neighborhood garden might be the proof in the experience of hours. These choices involve commitments, but they also
stretch time, because as you choose to spend time on these things,
you become in your mind the kind of person who *has* the time
to spend on these things. As a wealthy person allocates her capital
to different investments, you likewise allocate your resources in
pursuit of the returns you desire.

Indeed, I will argue in this book that the correlations in my
time-diary study that might seem straightforward—for example, people who feel like they have more time spend more time
doing reflective activities such as praying, meditating, or journaling than those who feel like they have less time—don't work
in the obvious direction. It is not that people who have more
free time have the time to reflect. After all, people with low
time-perception scores actually spend more time on social media and TV than people with high time-perception scores. Instead, people allocate time to thinking and reflecting, and *then
they feel that they have more time.*

Time is fluid, and these allocations may need to change in
different seasons. But being off the clock means dealing with
time on your terms. You are in control. Time is not something
to be feared, a steady drumbeat marching toward doom. It is
no more than an idea, to be studied and manipulated as an art-

ist might use her materials. Once you develop this mind-set of freedom, you can make choices to stretch time where you wish it to stretch. You can free it up where you wish to free it up. You can move tasks around to make more of them fit into your life than most people think is possible. You can deepen the experience of individual moments to the point where time almost seems to stand still.

The Start of a Journey

This book is about people with full lives who nonetheless see time as abundant. It is about how they structure their full lives to avoid time stress and feel better about the hours they have.

In sharing these strategies, I hope this book will help anyone who feels constantly behind, unsure how to escape what feels like an unchosen busyness. I hope it will encourage people to ask bigger questions of meaning and purpose, even though I know time management on its own does not seem like a profound topic. It is easy to see self-absorption in the subject, and small-mindedness too. We are spinning on an improbable planet in the middle of cold space. Headlines carry news of violence, cruelty, and disasters turning lives on end. Yet here we are, discussing how to turn a 60-minute meeting into a 45-minute one. There is privilege in believing that you can manage your time, and "privilege" often becomes an argument in itself, though I suspect it is as prevalent in the critics of time-management literature as it is in the proponents. Let us put it this way: if you have time to read essays about how modern people are not as busy as we think we are, and you have time to construct detailed rebuttals about just how busy you are, you are probably not starved for time either.

Instead, I think most of us want to do what we can to make the most of what we have been given. Learning to deal with time on your own terms is a process. It is for me. I am not the archetypal self-help narrator who has hit rock bottom and then experienced an epiphany on how to rescue myself and others. My life is not that interesting. Instead, I see myself as a student. I like to study the data. I like to challenge assumptions. I like to evaluate what goes right and wrong in each sphere of life with the goal of making tomorrow better than today.

Some days I don't see evidence of this progress. My failings go both directions. I am frantic because everything has gone wrong on the way out the door and I am late to the airport. Alternately, I have wasted hours online on a gorgeous spring afternoon scrolling through comments on an article that wasn't worth reading in the first place.

Some days, though, I do better. I shape my hours so I can have that open morning amid the boats in Bar Harbor, and then while running there I find a phrase turning over in my mind. That phrase becomes an idea for a book. The book represents a commitment of many hours, but they are hours spent joyfully, often even off the clock. Time is passing, yet not in a rush. For a while, it is more the pace of the waves lapping at that Maine shore: gentle, calm, serene.

THE SECRETS OF PEOPLE WITH ALL THE TIME IN THE WORLD

1. Tend your garden.

2. Make life memorable.

3. Don't fill time.

4. Linger.

5. Invest in your happiness.

6. Let it go.

7. People are a good use of time.

ONE

TEND YOUR GARDEN

Mindfulness gives you time. Time gives you choices.
Choices, skillfully made, lead to freedom.

—Bhante Henepola Gunaratana,
Beyond Mindfulness in Plain English

Robert Kauffman has been a school principal for twenty-one years. During that time, he's discovered a truth about education and, really, any field involving good intentions and infinite demands. "I think people are often just overwhelmed," he says. Being a principal is an "ambiguous" job, which lends itself to "winging it." A new school leader will feel compelled to focus on the crises right in front of her. The trouble is that, at the end of a crisis-filled day, she'll realize she never did check in with that teacher who wanted advice on reteaching a math concept few pupils understood. The urgent crowds out the important. The important doesn't get done.

Thanks to his two decades of experience, Kauffman imagined he was more effective than average, but in 2016, when he became the principal of Hillside Elementary School in Farmington Hills,

Michigan, he knew he would be challenged in new ways. The school had an outsized proportion of English-language learners. He wanted to find time to support his best teachers, and mentor those who needed help. He wanted to focus on improving student performance without getting derailed by every late bus and broken pipe.

So in late 2016, Kauffman signed on to the National SAM Innovation Project. This fascinating principal professional development program is centered on the belief that principal time is uniquely valuable. A teacher can influence the twenty-five students in his class. A principal can influence a whole school. But for principal time to be invested well, first the principal needs to know where his time goes. Then he can figure out options for redeploying time to the tasks that he does best. After that, he can do the hard work of following up daily to check that these lofty goals are reflected in the reality of how he spends his hours.

Kauffman, who calls himself a "data dork," was keen to get this information. After the principal did some initial work with SAM headquarters, a black-clad gentleman appeared at Hillside Elementary School to follow Kauffman around for a Monday-through-Friday school week. Like Kauffman's very own Boswell, the man recorded in five-minute increments absolutely everything Kauffman did. This included snacks and water breaks. He followed him into the lunchroom and into meetings. He made notes as Kauffman dealt with the plethora of discipline issues that of course cropped up during a week when teachers were conscious of creating a good impression. Kauffman had prepared the staff, though he notes that they were still deadly curious about the whole process. Some tried to engage the mysterious scribe in conversation, generally with no result (he was beholden to clean data!).

Soon thereafter, Kauffman received his stats. He learned that he was spending 39.2 percent of his time on "instructional leadership"—the teacher and curriculum management that tends to be the highest-value use of a principal's time. That's better than the average principal, who spends about 30 percent of her time on these matters, but less than Kauffman wanted. Time passes whether or not we think about how we spend it, and this is as true in an elementary school as it is anywhere else. Without active tending, Kauffman's time was easily taken over by the equivalent of weeds: dealing with paperwork that could be managed by other people, constantly answering email, and spending too much time supervising the cafeteria.

So, like a landscape designer surveying his plot, he sketched ideas of what he would like his time to look like. He brainstormed ways to be in the classrooms more often. He created "Teaching Tuesdays," during which he'd teach lessons to give teachers examples of techniques. Most worked, though some bombed, which was a learning experience for everyone. He designated times during which he would give teachers positive feedback. "I'm not a celebratory feedback guy," he confesses. "The joke is if I say it's okay, it means it's great," but lauding what goes right is curiously motivational.

With guidance from SAM headquarters, he aimed to build in thirty minutes a day for personal matters, such as making doctor appointments or calling contractors to get bids on home projects. Without dedicated time, these activities could bleed into the rest of the day and derail other goals. Or else they might not happen, creating work/life stress (more the case for Kauffman; his baseline was a mere 1.4 percent of time spent on anything remotely personal, including time in the bathroom). He also worked on not scheduling every minute. "You want to leave open space in your calendar," he says. That way, "whatever comes up comes up."

All this was exciting, but putting twenty minutes on the schedule to give a teacher celebratory feedback is helpful only if you then spend twenty minutes actually doing it. Things come up. Yet here's the reality of those interruptions and setbacks: If the fire alarm goes off during those scheduled twenty minutes, that doesn't change the fact that the feedback was a priority. Using time well means immediately rescheduling that feedback to a time that has been intentionally left open precisely because things like the fire alarm will happen.

During the six months after he tracked his time, Kauffman and an employee he designated to be his "school administration manager" (that's the "SAM" part of the program) checked in every day to see if his time was spent as it was supposed to be spent. If the previous day had gone off the rails, they tried to understand why. They analyzed what prevented Kauffman from spending time on the things only he could do. "I think the

single greatest thing of SAM is that a principal is held accountable for his time," he says. His SAM kept nudging him to make
time on his schedule to work with a teacher who really needed
guidance. They had identified this as a priority, so it was given
larger swaths of space than Kauffman might have naturally given
it. His SAM urged him to stop doing things, such as lunchroom
duty, that others could do. They figured out who could be a "first
responder" if a parent called about an issue that didn't need to
be escalated up the chain of command. "I was everywhere prior
to SAM," Kauffman says. "But we can't be everywhere, nor
should we be everywhere."

The result: a follow-up study at the end of the 2016–2017
school year found that Kauffman was spending 51 percent of his
time on instructional leadership. That's like gaining an additional twelve days of high-impact work time during the one
hundred days he spent on this calendar awareness. That time
had impact as teachers responded to Kauffman's focus on their
skills. The proportion of Hillside students demonstrating pro-
ficiency on state math tests rose by 4.2 percentage points that
year, with similar gains in reading.

None of this is easy; constantly minding time is more challenging than letting it slip unnoticed into the past. It is also
never done. Habits ("Teaching Tuesdays") help make good decisions automatic, yet there is never a moment when the time
thing is figured out. Six veteran teachers might decide to leave,
and a principal's time would then need to pivot to mentoring
the new ones. The school day might change. School demo-

graphics might change. This is why the constant evaluation is necessary.

Yet this labor—this discipline—can lead to a surprising mental lightening. J. Thomas Roth, principal of Reddick Elementary School in Hillsborough County, Florida, has also tracked and monitored his time through the National SAM Innovation Project. He notes that this attention "has upgraded my life all the way around. I'm more effective at school," he says, having massively increased the time he spends on instructional leadership of the teachers serving Reddick's mostly low-income population. But "it's rare that I'm there past 4:30 P.M. anymore. I can leave for the day knowing what I've accomplished." Knowing that he has time on tomorrow's schedule to work with a teacher who's concerned about classroom discipline, Roth can relax when he's with his family. He can go to the gym. Asking daily where his time should go and then knowing where his time has gone, he knows for sure that "we really get a lot of stuff done here. It gives you that affirmation that you're doing good things."

Where the Time Really Goes

Everyone has an obsession. As you have probably guessed a few thousand words into this book, time and how we spend it—including how *I* spend it—is mine. Here's something I know: to write the introductory story to this chapter, I interviewed Kauffman on Friday, July 14, 2017, from 1:00 to 1:30 P.M. That was a day in which I slept in until 6:45 A.M., spent forty-five minutes dealing with some school paperwork, and devoted thirty minutes in the late afternoon to making sure there were no bills in my giant pile of mail. I interviewed Roth on Friday, July 21, at 9:30 A.M., shortly after devoting thirty minutes to practicing a speech I was giving to interns in Washington, D.C., the next week. That day also featured an afternoon phone call with my editor for this book—albeit about a different project—and a big-kids-only evening excursion from 6:15 to 8:30 P.M., inclusive of travel time, to Benihana.

I know these things not because I can remember all the stupid trivia of my life, but because, like Kauffman and Roth, I have tracked my time—in my case, continually, for several years. At first, I simply wanted to know where my time went. I assumed I could write about the numbers for my blog.

But as time went on, this experiment in mindfulness became so much more than that. The daily discipline of minding one's hours, I learned, changes the experience of time. It can lead to a savored life. As famed landscape architect Beatrix Farrand once said of a different sort of cultivation, "It is work—hard work, and at the same time it is perpetual pleasure."

Time, it turns out, is like Farrand's expertise: gardens—like the garden that I look at daily through my office window, watching the progression from daffodils in March to asters in the fall. Because it is my family's garden, I know the work of which Farrand speaks. I have watched my husband weed, water, and replace plants that pests kill. Any given weekend sees him pruning the rosebushes or planting mums. He likes the work—well, except for that one time when a chain saw tree-trimming accident sent him to the ER—which is why he has never farmed it out. The gardener just has to accept that gardening is not a set-it-and-forget-it activity. You assess, you tweak. You learn that even the hardiest plants have vulnerabilities. In early 2017, a few warm February days sent the buds on our magnolia tree into production. Then a March blizzard thwarted this growth, and those gorgeous cotton candy blossoms never opened. But this vigilance, and the setbacks, can be balanced with moments of enjoyment too. Indeed, it is the vigilance that leads to summer evenings when I sit on the back porch, look out at the crepe myrtles, and think, *Wow*.

Likewise, with time, it is the same process. A gardener must know his plot. He must think about what he wants it to look like. Then it is the daily cultivation that leads to beauty, in a landscape and a life too. As the Buddhist monk and meditation teacher Bhante Henepola Gunaratana writes in his book *Beyond Mindfulness in Plain English*, "Mindfulness gives you time. Time gives you choices. Choices, skillfully made, lead to freedom." Knowing where my time goes, and choosing to tend my schedule as one might tend a garden, has changed my life, just as the same process has changed life for teachers and students at the Hillside and Reddick schools. It has made me feel like I have more time, like my schedule is surprisingly open. I believe it will make your life feel lighter too.

This chapter is about how to achieve such freedom. It is about how to attain the sort of skilled and blossoming mindfulness that lets you go off the clock.

My 8,784 Hours

But back to my story—the tale of how I created a record of my July principal interviews and that Benihana trip. A confluence of events led to my decision, in April 2015, to become my own Boswell, recording my time in half-hour chunks. I had had hundreds of people track their time for me for various projects over the years, and I had tracked my own time for a dozen weeks here and there. As a born skeptic, I had long been fascinated by what these logs showed about the blind spots people have about time. There can be great gaps between how we think we spend our time and reality as recorded. People claim to have no leisure time and then can recount in detail what happened on the most recent *Big Bang Theory*. Or—I was guilty of this one—we feel like we spend hours unloading the dishwasher, only to learn it takes five minutes each time, the four times per week we do it.

I didn't think I'd have many glaring blind spots, but I was curious about my time. I had fallen off the wagon of keeping a journal, and I suspected, that April, that I was about to live through a watershed few years of my life. In mid-May 2014, shortly before Jasper's seventh birthday, I had woken one morning to an unexpected but familiar wave of nausea. A pregnancy test and a doctor visit confirmed that my fourth child was on his way.

Alex was born in January 2015. Going from three children to four is less shocking than going from zero to one, but newborns are always challenging, and caring for a newborn along with a seven-year-old, five-year-old, and three-year-old was going to test my organizational skills. Around the same time, my work life was taking some exciting turns. *I Know How She Does It,* my book on how professional women make the most of their time, was going to be published in June 2015. My speaking calendar for the next year was filling up. As I spoke to audiences about how people made their lives work, I wanted to see in as factual a way as possible how I did it.

So, fully back at work three months after the birth of my fourth child, I opened a new spreadsheet on Monday, April 20, 2015. I started filling in the cells, which ran from 5:00 A.M. to 4:30 A.M. on the vertical axis, with the days of the week across the top. There wasn't a big gap before the first waking entry. I was up at 5:30 A.M. to nurse Alex, something I would do five times that day, with a sixth feeding coming from a pumped bottle. I took Jasper to the bus stop. I had a conference call with the publicity team at my publisher. I sat outside enjoying the spring blossoms while the baby napped in the evening. I made it into bed around 10:00 P.M. The next day, I chaperoned Sam's field trip to a local museum, then I took the train to New York City for some professional events. I made it home at 10:30 P.M., and chatted with my husband before pumping and going to bed at 11:30 P.M., to rise at 5:45 A.M. the next day and start again.

I soon fell into a rhythm of tracking. Each Monday morning, I'd fill in the conclusion of Sunday, and archive that week's log. Then I'd open a new sheet. I'd fill in my log every few hours. That was easy enough on workdays when I was at my computer. On weekends, the need to record my hours drove more traffic into my home office than I felt was ideal. So I learned how to remember what I was doing. I'd jot down notes on paper if necessary, and soon I was able to reconstruct twenty-four hours with reasonable accuracy. I was OK with broad categories. "Work" occupying a half hour might mean various projects, but generalizing meant time tracking took only three minutes or so daily. While that adds up to twenty-one minutes per week—a bit more than eighteen hours per year—that's roughly the amount of time I spend brushing my teeth annually, an activity I've not seen reason to question.

That summer, fall, winter, spring, I continued. My time log bore witness to an eleven-hour drive out to the Indiana Dunes, and the mad chase to catch a feral cat that followed us into our vacation rental and leaped into the crib with Alex, sending them both screaming into the air. It testified to copious quantities of time spent pumping breast milk. It recorded trips to Chicago, London, and Orlando. I wrote down the times I drove Jasper to swim practice or drove Sam home from Lego club. And yes, in case you're wondering, intimate activities made it on the time log too, described euphemistically so I could keep printed logs lying about, even if handymen or inquisitive children came into my office.

As mid-April came again—a time characterized by a brutal stomach bug that led to hours of laundry—I wrote on my blog that I'd share the totals shortly. I assumed this would be of little interest to anyone who wasn't already reading updates on LauraVanderkam.com. So I was shocked when, one night as my family was waiting to eat at Uno Pizzeria & Grill, I checked my email and found a query from an editor at the *New York Times* asking if I might be interested in writing about my time tracking for them. I may have waited fifteen seconds to respond. This prospect of a much (much) bigger audience than had ever found its way to my corner of the internet added fire to getting my totals right.

I spent the next two weeks surrounded by spreadsheets of what would normally be 8,760 hours but with the leap year was 8,784 hours. Having been most concerned about the numbers, my first step was to page through everything and type numbers into my calculator. But as I made it to the analysis stage, several surprising facts jumped out at me.

My essay ran in the Sunday Review section in mid-May with the headline "The Busy Person's Lies," and indeed this close attention to my time revealed many lies I had been telling myself. Even *I* had my stories. Ultimately, though, the truth is liberating. It opened up space for me to ask what I wanted my life to look like, and how I could make changes in my day-to-day existence that would make me feel like I had more time than I thought possible.

The Blind Spots

My first false story was a particularly painful one. In my speeches, I love to highlight a study finding that people claiming 75-plus-hour workweeks are overestimating by an average of twenty-five hours. I recount the young man who once told me about his 180-hour workweeks, which is impressive for being twelve more hours than a week actually contains. In the weeks I had tracked over the years, I had consistently worked about fifty hours a week, and so I thought this was my number. Unlike everyone else, *I* was immune to exaggeration.

But when I tracked for a year, I saw that in the past, I had chosen very specific weeks to track: namely, weeks when I worked fifty hours, because *I wanted to see myself as the kind of person who worked fifty hours a week.*

Tracking all my weeks removed that possibility. I saw that—even subtracting vacations—my tally was right at forty that first year. Forty is a different number than fifty. In my mental model of life there were ten more hours devoted to one category than the long-term average showed. Certainly some weeks I worked fifty hours. Some weeks I worked sixty hours. But in my effort to convince myself that I was the sort of serious professional who worked long hours, because I believed that serious professionals must work long hours, I had done the same mental gymnastics as everyone else. I remembered my longest weeks as typical. I dismissed other weeks as atypical even though they were no more atypical than the long ones.

Of course, if I was working forty hours a week, not fifty, that left open the question of where the other ten hours were going. I knew from studying other people's time logs that the culprits in this time seepage are varied: inefficient transitions, puttering around the house while waiting for things to stop or start, diving into online rabbit holes.

In my case, the kids accounted for a lot of my time, but to my surprise, I spent nine hours weekly on housework and errands. That is lower than the average for a working mother whose youngest child is under age six (the American Time Use Survey pegs this at about eighteen hours per week), but it isn't as low as it could have been. I also spent more than seven hours each week in the car. This number shocked me, because I work out of my home office. I have no daily commute, so "time in the car" wasn't registering as a large category. But between driving the kids, meeting people, driving to the airport, and running around doing errands, I spent more time in the car than I did reading or exercising. Another shocking realization: the CD player in my car had been broken for much of the year, thwarting my ambition to listen to musical masterworks. This meant that week after week I had spent one of my precious hours per day listening to Sirius XM radio's The Pulse or The Blend. No wonder I knew so many Andy Grammer songs by heart.

I exercised for 233 hours, or about 4.4 hours weekly. It was sobering to see that even in the weeks of training for the three half marathons I ran that first year, this tally didn't go up much. Exercise takes a lot of time only in our explanations of why we're not doing it.

I read for 327 hours. That sounds great—nearly an hour a day—though I was puzzled at the end of the first year to see how few good books that encompassed. I later calculated that I read at a pace of roughly fifty to sixty pages per hour, so those hours could have represented 16,350–19,620 pages. That's enough to plow through *War and Peace*, *1Q84*, *Kristin Lavransdatter*, and the other doorstops on my reading bucket list. Let's just say that did not happen. Instead, I read a lot of magazines, my form of mindless entertainment (I watched TV a mere fifty-seven hours that first year). There is nothing noble in reading a story about how air-popped popcorn is a great low-calorie snack or, worse, gossip about actors on TV shows rather than watching the TV shows themselves, so this was a category to be improved upon.

Because I had a baby—who did not sleep well—sleep became a subject of intense interest. Before time tracking, I might have been tempted to claim sleep deprivation. Indeed, my sleep was disjointed; I was woken up 146 nights at some point before 4:30 A.M. that first year to deal with something (generally a kid). Alex took longer than his siblings had to settle into a good sleep schedule.

But if the sleep didn't always happen at the times I wanted, the totals had an uncanny consistency. The first year I averaged

7.4 hours of sleep per day. After I passed that first April, I decided to keep going and track a second year. Sure enough, the second year I tracked I averaged . . . 7.4 hours per day. The average was the same to within one one-hundredth of an hour (less than a minute) year after year. This does not mean I slept 7.4 hours *each day*, or even that I hit 51.8 hours weekly. My range was 47–57 hours per week that first year, and 46–56 hours the second. But over any long stretch of time, my body aimed for 7.4 hours daily. I could see the catching up on my logs. A bad week meant I would nap on the weekends instead of reading magazines during the baby's nap time. I would crash at 9:30 P.M. A few nights of a 9:30 P.M. bedtime would put me back on track, and then I'd stay up late again, until I once more felt the need to catch up.

Another area of shocking consistency: those euphemistically labeled intimate encounters. My tallies of such encounters (and I'll presume my husband's) for April 20, 2015, to April 19, 2016, and then April 20, 2016, to April 19, 2017, were exactly the same. Not close. *The same.* We don't schedule these things for certain times, and the yearly totals were high enough into the three figures that this seems improbable. And yet, I did the math. Apparently this was the level of intimacy that felt right, or at least felt doable while the children were distracted with video games.

Mindfulness Gives You Time

I found tracking useful enough that I kept going after the second April as well. I like looking back over the spreadsheets.

Memories help stretch time, and having records of our lives solidifies memories. I wouldn't naturally spend time pondering that July Benihana trip, but once I see it on my log, the details come back: the Japanese marble soda that two of the children liked and one hated, the edamame one would eat and the other two would not, the kids' paper chef hats that dangled perilously close to the flaming grill. I was more relaxed than usual about my children being near an open fire thanks to a glass of rosé that was advertised as going well with Japanese food. I made a note of that dinner, and now I can recall more of these moments than if I had not recorded them. These details expand the hours that made up my past.

I find this forced mindfulness to be a good thing. Time passes whether or not we think about how we are spending it. Tracking forces me to think about it. But when I mention my time-tracking habit to people—that I know how I spent every half hour of the past several years—I get nervous laughter. Perhaps people worry I'm about to bore them with a recitation. Or perhaps the person was about to ask for time-management advice and realizes if that is going to be the advice, better to change the subject.

So I want to be clear: no one needs to track her time for two years, or even two months, though I do think two weeks is a good goal. Maybe that could include a "typical" week and an "atypical" week, just to see what varies and what does not.

But many people do not want to track time at all. If I get an explanation, the reasons fall into two categories. The first is that a time log will show how much time the person is wasting—just as a food log reveals an I-swear-it's-only-a-few-chips habit—and that is not really a reason, at least in the sense of being unique to that person. We all waste time. I know I do. I putter around the kitchen and read clickbait headlines when I should go to bed. People will sit on a conference call that has been scheduled to take thirty minutes but has run out of steam after five, asking, "So, what else do we need to cover?" It is the human condition to spend precious hours as if they were plentiful on things that are neither enjoyable nor meaningful to us or the people we care about.

The second reason, though, is more complex. It is one I've grappled with as I think about my time. People claim they don't have time to track time, which is patently false. What they mean is that they don't *want* to track time, usually because they feel that being cognizant of all their time would make them feel anxious or overly preoccupied with their minutes. Their lives would be tethered to lines on a spreadsheet. They know, as I know, that the best moments of life are when we are *not* watching the time, such as when we are reading a good book and not even noticing until midnight has come and gone. They, like I, love to feel off the clock.

I agree that such off-the-clock moments are lovely. I also know that in any full life, the clock is always going to creep into the picture eventually. A major client schedules a meeting for 7:30 A.M. The flight to Nashville leaves at 4:40 P.M., you live thirty minutes from the airport, and you have to account for waits to get through security. The dry cleaner closes at 6:30 P.M. and you're out of clean shirts.

Most of us *already* have to be accountable for our time. The reason to try tracking time is that even extremely busy people often have some space they can redeploy for enjoyable, meaningful things. A physician discovers she can compress her Friday afternoon administrative work and slip out early for a run in Central Park. A real estate broker sees he can respond to emails at set times, and he opens up space for thinking about how he'll build his business.

As with the principals tracking their time, it is this second step, envisioning how a schedule could look, and the third step, holding yourself daily to this design, that leads to time freedom.

New Habits

I know it is this redeployment, and my new habits, that changed my perception of time. I looked at the numbers from my first year of tracking and made several changes.

First, if I was working forty hours a week rather than fifty, I needed to make the most of those forty hours. I became more strategic about which articles I chose to write. I nudged up my speaking rates. As I looked at my day-to-day choices, I realized that I was sometimes running errands during prime work hours. It felt like a break and the stores were empty. I would also drive the school-aged children to activities in the afternoons. The former I decided I could outsource. The latter I decided not to, or at least not completely (shuttling around four kids often requires multiple drivers anyway). Ultimately, being the kind of parent who will pick up a kid from swim practice at 5:20 P.M. on a workday, eat dinner with the crew, and then take off for wrestling at 6:20 P.M. means my work hours will be limited. But—and this was a breakthrough—I also realized that I could challenge my stories. Even if I was only working forty hours a week, I was doing a lot with those forty hours. I was meeting my goals. I was exceeding my goals. Did "fifty" matter for anything beyond my ego?

I decided I could embrace a lower number. Indeed, in the second year of tracking, I let the number drift down more, to thirty-five hours per week. I allocated those five extra hours to daytime adventures, the sort that let me feel off the clock, as I'd go to a noon organ recital at a nearby church or visit a wine-tasting room after I'd given a speech in Napa.

With solo time in the car, I began taking my own advice. I started packing more listening material, particularly podcasts, on my phone. I got so into podcasts that when one of my favorite bloggers, Sarah Hart-Unger, posted on The SHU Box that she was thinking of starting a podcast, I reached out and suggested we launch one together. Within a month, I could play episodes of our joint venture, *Best of Both Worlds*, while I drove to the airport.

As for my addiction to magazine reading, I realized by year two that I would read more books in those 327 annual reading hours if books were easy to read and I always had a good idea of what I should read next. I built book planning and buying into my life. I dedicated thirty minutes every two to three weeks to reading reviews, following Amazon's algorithms, or buying whatever Modern Mrs. Darcy (www.ModernMrsDarcy.com) was recommending. I installed the Kindle app on my phone. That nudged me to turn headline-scrolling time or social-media-perusal time into book-reading time. I began keeping a log of books read, and relished seeing the list grow.

Soon enough, my gossip magazine totals fell. I began reading literature in earnest, including titles I've long meant to read, such as Willa Cather's "prairie trilogy" and lesser-known works by Hemingway, Fitzgerald, Wharton, et al. During the month of August 2017, I actually made it through both *Kristin Lavransdatter* and *1Q84*. That required about forty hours of reading, which, spread over thirty-one days, isn't that much more than I was doing before. But it was time spent mindfully, not mindlessly. It was about my learning to note when I had open time, and then choosing to pick up a book rather than something else. This took more effort than spending time on less challenging things, but realizing I had the freedom to read like a graduate student as the working mother of four children was absolutely liberating.

Finding Free Time

Other busy people from all walks of life have discovered—through persistent time tracking—that they have space in their schedules too. In May 2017, I received an email from a young man named Drew Paul, who was then a sophomore finance major at Loyola University Chicago. He told me that he'd been assigned to track his time for a leadership course and then, being the high achiever I soon realized he was, he decided to track the entire sixteen weeks of the spring semester. He logged time devoted to classes and studying, to sleep, to internship hunting, and to his fraternity, where he served as the recruitment chair. He calculated weekly totals. Then he looked to see whether he was under or over his targets, and why.

He learned several things as he looked at the early weeks. First, TV took more time than he liked. "I definitely tried to cut out the amount of Netflix I was watching," he says, and he soon knocked this down from about twelve hours per week to six. He also realized that his fraternity was quite a commitment. Rush events consumed fifty-two hours one week, between planning and interviews and the social events themselves. "It was kind of ridiculous," he says, if rewarding to make new friends. "I was expecting it would take twenty hours, but that was just a guess. I'd never done it before."

Fortunately that calmed down once the new members were in, and he realized that he had developed a lot of good habits too. He was dedicated to getting his sleep; even during rush week he got himself home and to bed by 1:00 A.M. each night. And he saw that he was diligent enough with studying that he could relax. "I realized that I do really have a lot more time than I thought," he says. He was willing to chat with me on a Wednesday during finals week, and he told me that he had gone out with friends the previous night, despite having two finals scheduled that weekend. "I didn't feel bad about going out because I had put in five hours at the library [on Tuesday]," he says. It was right there on the time log. He could also see that he would log more hours on Thursday and Friday before his finals, and he could look back over the semester and see all the previously invested hours. "It made me realize I could fit in other things," he says. "It made me feel better. I can do this because I worked efficiently previously." That's a better feeling than the usual finals panic that has people pulling all-nighters.

Claudia André, another time tracker, likewise had the happy realization that she didn't have to be up all night, albeit for very different reasons. André, a lawyer, already had two young children when, embarking on the project of having a third, she and her husband spontaneously conceived triplets. This sort of surprise might seem to consume all available space. Indeed, the literature André found on raising multiples was profoundly negative. She was warned that she would never sleep or have time for herself again.

A curious person, she wondered if this would be true. She decided to track her time for a week at three different junctures in the triplets' lives: at seven months, twelve months, and eighteen months.

During that first week she logged, conditions were tough. She slept six hours a night. "That's not great, but it's not terrible either," she says. Since her triplets were born almost three months prematurely, their development at seven months was equivalent to a full-term baby's development at four months, and many infants don't sleep through the night at that point. "I would assume there are other moms of four-month-olds who get that amount of sleep and only have one baby." Still, she managed to get about two hours of personal time per day, which she used to read, shop, watch TV, and go to the gym. (She wound up taking a break from legal work during this time, with the intention of returning when the triplets were a little older.) She worked on her blog, The Type A Mom of Multiples, and visited with her sister. With the help of a babysitter, she visited her older two children's schools as well.

By the second week she tracked, a year after her babies were born, she had made several changes that helped improve conditions. By getting the triplets on a solid nap and bedtime schedule, she was managing to score 7.5 hours of sleep per day. She had gained an additional half hour daily of personal time. By the third week she tracked, life was opening up a lot. She was still sleeping about the same—7.4 hours per day despite her preference for eight—but "the triplets were not the reason I wasn't getting more sleep," she says. She was often staying up later by choice to chat with her husband or do things around the house. She was also averaging about three hours per day of personal time, or twenty-one hours a week.

Given that many people without triplets claim to have nowhere near this amount of space, I find this impressive. To be sure, this doesn't mean that caring for multiples is easy, or that all parents of multiples will have the same experience. Some triplets have more profound medical issues, and for André, achieving this amount of free time required incredible mindfulness about her schedule, and constantly evaluating what was working and what was not, but her takeaway was: "I do have time in the day for myself—I just have to be clear on my priorities. Sometimes it's good to just take a step back and see that I am in control of what I do, and if I am spending time on something I want to be spending time on, that's good." Overall, "I have been pleasantly surprised at how delightful—and dare I say manageable?—it is to have triplets. I deeply regret not having more encouragement and optimism about my future with triplets, so through my blog, I hope to change that possibility for someone else."

Designing a "Realistic Ideal Day"

If you'd like to try tracking time as I do, and as Paul and André did, you can get a time log template through the subscription form on my website. It's a simple investment in your happiness; in my time-perception survey, I found that people who strongly agreed with the statement "Yesterday, I felt like I had a good sense of where my time went" were 21 percent more likely than average to say that they had made progress toward their personal or professional goals in the previous twenty-four hours. Once you know where the time goes, it becomes easier to ask where you'd like it to go to create the life you'd like.

That said, I know not everyone reading this will try tracking. Not everyone who starts will stick with it for a week, let alone for longer. There are enough diet books whose sole selling point is that "you don't have to count calories!" that I know such things seem tedious. Also, many successful people do not track their time. Some do for work, but it is the rare person who tracks everything. (Indeed, the SAM principals looked only at their work time and any personal time that happened while they were in their school buildings.)

So, yes, it is possible to tend your garden without tracking all 168 hours a week for the rest of your life. While knowing where the time goes is fascinating, it is the envisioning of how you would like to spend your time, and then the day-to-day evaluation and tweaking, that truly matters for spending time better.

Courtney Westlake, an author and copywriter based in Springfield, Illinois, tells me that she imagines what a "realistic ideal day" would look like. (Not a "perfect day." Though that can be a fun exercise, that's more of a long-term question. A realistic ideal day must work within the framework of your current life.)

During the realistic ideal day Westlake designed recently, she included reading time for herself, and reading time with her kids. She'd work on an important professional project; she'd take a hot bath. She and her husband would spend quality time together not staring at their phones. "Not every day is of course going to look like that," she says, but "how can I strive to make that happen as much as possible?"

It's a smart question, and there's no reason to stop at just a realistic ideal day. How about a whole realistic ideal week? What would you do with your hours?

Even if you don't think about every minute, pondering the big things you'd like to see happen in the forthcoming week is smart. After all, a week is the cycle of life as we live it. Monday and Sunday look different, but both occur just as often. One isn't more typical than the other. I find the best time to do this weekly planning session is on Friday afternoons. If you work a Monday through Friday schedule, most likely you are not doing much of consequence by Friday after lunch. It's hard to start anything new as you slide toward the weekend, but you can think about what your future self should be doing. This can turn what would be wasted time into the most productive afternoon of the week.

I started doing this Friday planning a few years ago, and I find it helpful for keeping me focused on what matters. I carve out a few minutes to look at the next week, and make myself a three-category priority list:

- Career

- Relationships

- Self

What would I most like to accomplish in each area over the next week? The list can be short, just two or three items in each. The career category might contain writing the draft of a new speech and setting up meetings for an upcoming trip. The relationships category might include dinner out with my husband and running with a friend. The self category could be scheduling a dentist appointment and seeing an exhibit at a local museum. Then I can look at the calendar for the next week and write in these priorities.

If each one requires multiple steps, I can make these steps part of my intentions for each day, which is another way people can tend their gardens. For any given day, think about what three things are most important for you to do. If you knew the power in your office or home was going to go out at 11:00 A.M., what would you be racing to get done before then?

Identifying priorities helps me make sure important things get done, but what I've been most startled by is how much *time* this planning opens up. Even big things don't take long when they are identified and broken down into steps. Ideally, I front-load these steps to the start of the week. It is dizzying to accomplish your most important business goals for the week by the end of Monday. Then the rest of the week can feel off the clock rather than like a mad dash to get some nebulous quantity of unknown stuff done by Friday night.

You can also tend your garden by looking backward. At night, take a few moments to write a daily reflection in a journal. Answer a few questions:

- What did I like most about today?

- What would I like to have spent more time doing?

- What would I like to have spent less time doing?

- How can I make that happen?

Sometimes when people ask these questions they decide to make big changes. An engineer wrote me recently that she had studied her schedule and realized that she was not thrilled enough with her job to justify the two hours she spent commuting each day. Her manager tolerated her working from home once a week, if that. So she interviewed for and was offered a different job that was more flexible and closer to home. She shared this news with her current manager. Her manager decided that if she would stay, he would become comfortable with her working from home four days per week. Just like that, hours opened up, whether she took the new job or stayed with the old one.

Taking Charge

When some people look at their schedules, they decide much is good. This should be celebrated. But whether life needs a little work or a lot of work, tending your metaphorical garden always comes back to this: ownership.

This is true in real gardens, a fact that any visitor to Central Park in the past three decades has seen. In the late 1970s, this public space was in a state of total decay. Benches were broken. Meadows had become dust bowls. Graffiti and garbage led to a sense that the park wasn't being watched, and violent crime predictably followed. The park wasn't understaffed. More than three hundred Parks Department employees took care of Central Park's 843 acres. The problem was that there was little accountability. Someone mowing the grass might spot a drainage problem, or bad sight lines that allowed for criminal activity, but this park employee would have no easy way to report the issue up the chain of command and see it fixed.

This changed when the Central Park Conservancy, a public-private partnership that took over management of the park in the 1980s, instituted a system of master gardeners. Central Park is now divided into forty-nine geographic zones, each managed by a zone gardener who supervises grounds workers and volunteers. These master gardeners fully own the state of their plots. If there is a problem, it is their problem. They solve it. The result is a safe, beautiful urban oasis that people want to linger in, even after the sun goes down.

So it goes with lives. Becoming your life's master gardener means deciding that you are responsible for how you spend your time. It means believing that much of time is a choice.

This mind-set can change everything, even if its achievement requires wisdom and discipline. It is tempting to assign responsibility to someone or something else. I can't do X because of Y. Y might be a good reason. If you're sitting in a jail cell without writing materials, it will be difficult to use those hours to write a novel. Shocks—much like the March 2017 deep freeze that kept my trees from blooming—can tear into the best ordered life. We cannot control illnesses, layoffs, accidents. Life can be horribly unfair. If we think of our hours as gardens, we might realize that some of us, through no personal merit, have been born into wormy plots of Pennsylvania earth. Others have, through no fault of their own, been dealt dusty or root-filled patches. People have varying resources. Plenty of mugs and T-shirts bear the slogan "You have the same number of hours in the day as Beyoncé," to which wags have pointed out that she can leverage her hours through her wealth and connections in ways the rest of us cannot.

Or there's this more pedestrian constraint on time: people need varying amounts of sleep. As I saw from my time log, over the long term, my body *will* hit 7.4 hours per day. If I cut this short too many days in a row, I'll crash early, or catch naps when I can. I can move sleep around, but averaged over a period of a few months, I cannot escape that 7.4-hour daily requirement. It is perfectly normal to need between 6.5 hours and 8.5 hours of sleep per day, but compared with someone who needs 6.5 hours, someone who needs 8.5 hours gets two fewer hours per day to play around with. Over three years, someone needing 6.5 hours of sleep per day could work an entire extra work year versus someone who needed 8.5 hours per day, without losing a second of personal or family time.

This is all true, and yet not really an argument against ownership. It is easy to believe our own excuses, particularly if they're good ones, but in a world of 7 billion people, there is always *someone* facing Y who is doing X. All of us have to assess the plot of life we are allotted every twenty-four hours and figure out how we can make the most of what we've been given.

This is true for people in strained circumstances, and it is true for people with unfathomable resources. I don't think the process is automatic for anyone. When Oprah Winfrey interviewed J. K. Rowling about her schedule as she was writing the seventh Harry Potter book, Rowling spouted this little gem: "As I was finishing *Deathly Hallows* there came a day where the window cleaner came, the kids were at home, the dogs were barking, and I could not work, and this lightbulb went on over my head and I thought, *I can throw money at this problem. I can now solve this problem.*" So she decamped to a hotel to finish her draft. This is sensible, but think about the implications: it took her six bestselling books and a billion dollars to realize that her hours should be spent doing what only she could do. *None of us* is born with an operating manual for life.

But here's something we do all have: 24 hours in a day, 168 hours in a week. Whatever our constraints—our own or those that come from caring for others—by tending our gardens, we come closer, day by day, to building the lives we want in the time we've got.

Mindfulness gives you time. Time gives you choices. Choices lead to freedom, whatever one's plot of earth looks like. It is easy to fall into false narratives of time poverty, but choosing to change your story from "I'm too busy" to "I have time for what matters to me" can make you see possibilities. In time, such possibilities can make any garden bloom.

That's what Courtney Westlake (who designed her "realistic ideal day") discovered. Her second child, Brenna, was born with a rare skin condition called harlequin ichthyosis, in which her body produces excess skin. Skin has functions that most of us take for granted, and this genetic disorder has profound consequences. Brenna can't sweat, so her body temperature has to be carefully regulated. She's highly susceptible to infections. Her skin grows tight around her joints, which limits her movement. Indeed, her skin grew so thick over her fingers in the womb that she could not uncurl them for a long time. She doesn't grow much hair, and her skin is usually red enough that people do a double take. She needs a long bath daily to scrub the excess skin away, and must be covered head to toe in Aquaphor multiple times per day to keep her skin from cracking. She wakes most nights because she is so itchy; Westlake and her husband take turns soothing her and getting her back down.

The management of her condition requires regular medical and therapy appointments. Westlake reports that Brenna has eight different physicians she sees: an ENT to clean out the skin that grows thick in her ears and can keep her from hearing, dermatologists for the skin issues themselves, ophthalmologists for her various eye problems (such as being born without functional eyelids, which also turn out to be skin), a GI doctor (she had a feeding tube for the first few years of life), a rheumatologist to deal with her juvenile arthritis, and of course the general pediatrician for the routine kid stuff.

To say that caring for a special-needs child takes time is an understatement. Even on a weekend day when everyone might want to relax or go on adventures, the family has to figure out when Brenna can have her hour-long bath, and when she can get covered in lotion. A doctor's appointment means a twenty to thirty minute drive, then time in the waiting room, plus the visit itself. Westlake, as Brenna's primary caregiver, deals with the majority of this. For a while, when Brenna was a baby, it felt all-consuming. She could feel a victim mentality creeping in.

Yet at some point, she made a decision. She could keep grieving about what could not be, or she could assess her garden as it was and make what she could of it.

She chose to do the latter. When Brenna was three years old, Westlake reached out to me with the somewhat startling news that she too had more time than she might have thought. She had begun blogging about Brenna shortly after the girl's birth, partly to keep her far-flung cheering squad updated, and over time the blog led to a book contract. Westlake kept a time log for me, and while it showed vast quantities of time caring for her small children—"I spend SO much time with my kids. Too much time. Do you ever have anyone say that?!"—she had scored a few hours a day to work on the book that became *A Different Beautiful,* by hiring sitters and working during Brenna's nap. Her realistic ideal day included reading in the bathtub, and she managed to do that five times during the week she logged. She visited her in-laws. She helped out with childcare when a friend had a baby. She went to her husband's company picnic and watched a movie with him. She went to an awards dinner and to the pool with her older child. Then there was this hour-long spot of Monday-evening spontaneity: "Drive to get gas, see rainbow so we chase it." A few words on a spreadsheet evoke children in the backseat, faces pressed against the glass, laughing and yelling *This way, Mommy!* as they cruise down the rain-soaked streets.

Any garden can be tended, and in time even more space can open up. When I circled back with Westlake in early 2017, Brenna was in preschool five mornings a week, during which Westlake was scaling up her new writing career. In the fall, Brenna would go to kindergarten from 8:00 A.M. to 3:00 P.M., and with her productivity skills honed through years of making do, Westlake was "already starting to think about how I will structure that time so I don't squander it." She had big plans. Life was full of promise. She was tending her garden, and it was blooming like Pennsylvania in spring. Westlake reported that she had read fifty-eight books in 2016. "People say, 'How in the world did you find time for that?' I *made* time," she says. "I can choose the activities that fill me up internally instead of deplete me. I do have time to do what I want."

TWO

MAKE LIFE MEMORABLE

*Very often when we remark, "How did time fly
by so quickly?" what's actually meant is some version
of "I don't remember where the time went."*

—Alan Burdick, *Why Time Flies*

Time travel seems like the stuff of science fiction. Yet the human brain has a curious capacity for such voyages. Sit quietly and your consciousness travels somewhere, often somewhere in the past. Artifacts direct this travel in startling ways. I pull a book from the shelf and a receipt falls out. August 2002. I am suddenly back on the overnight train from Bangkok to a port on the coast of Thailand. I can feel the train rumbling beneath me as I walk through the sleeping compartments in the darkness.

This memory is incredibly vivid, yet the vividness is puzzling. I know I have not consciously thought of this scene in years. Where was this all stored, to be so easily pulled to the present?

"Memory is indeed mysterious," says Liz Currin, a clinical

psychologist who spends her working hours probing stories of her clients' pasts. Most people have memories dating from around age three. Others have no memories until much later in life, which is often a side effect of childhood trauma. The wounded brain buries things deep to protect itself, building up layers until the soil appears smooth. But in all people, telling details eventually poke their way to the surface. As with my receipt, it doesn't take much. "It could be a song, for instance," says Currin. "The most powerful of our senses in terms of evoking a memory appears to be the olfactory one." One whiff of honeysuckle and I remember a cheap perfume I happened upon as a teenager. It is a heady scent; it was a heady time.

For most of us, this mental travel is close to random. But Currin, knowing the power of memory, carefully evokes it to deepen her own sense of the past. She has two girls, Elyse and Sarah. They are now grown and off living their own lives. So "I frequently indulge myself in memories of them [as children] by imagining a treasure chest," she says. "When I open it, it is overflowing with beautiful jewels and gems, all sorts of colors and shapes. I'll reach into the chest and pick up one stone. I hold it in my hands, turn it over, relish the feeling and the beauty of it."

One particular memory that she returns to often is of taking her very young daughters to the neighborhood pool. The day is warm and sunny. She recalls many details: getting them into their bathing suits, slathering them with sunscreen, packing up pool toys, and then loading the entire entourage into the car.

She notes the humor at this point in the narrative: for such invasion-of-a-country level of preparation, the drive was all of a block and a half.

They swam; they came home. There was a fruit cup, putting things in the washing machine, a story, and a nap. It is "nothing remarkable," she notes. Still, "it is one of my most treasured memories." It has lingered in her mind as that summer turned to autumn, and then as more summers turned to autumns. Days go by. Years go by. Yet even if these splashing girls have drifted down the stream of time into the past, "I can return to the treasure chest any time I want," Currin says. The frequent polishing of such memories "keeps me closely connected to my daughters in their earliest years."

The treasure chest is a lovely image. It is one I like evoking as I think of what jewels exist from my own early days and the ones I am placing in the treasure chest of time now. My first memory is probably from around the age of three. I am a small child in this hazy recollection, and I am receiving a tea set. I must have been amazed by those tiny china cups if this image, of all possible images, is extant from that time. In another memory, I am singing a solo in a Christmas service at White Memorial Presbyterian Church. I was five years old. I wore a big red bow with my choir robe. I recall being in front of the church, looking out at the two sides of pews and the balcony, and singing the third verse of "Away in a Manger."

The intensity of such things—joy, performance—adds weight to memory. It is probably not random that these images are anchored in my brain. Memories get shaped to form a story, and the stories become who we are.

But these stories are not just interesting for psychologists seeking clues to our current dilemmas. The existence of memories turns out to have profound implications for how we feel about time: whether it is scarce or abundant, whether it feels full or like it has slipped through our fingers. Often, we treat memory as more filing cabinet than treasure chest. We assume things are stored automatically, as they exist, even if we know the papers fade as time goes on.

Yet people who have a holistic perspective on these matters know that memory is more than that. What goes in as raw material can be polished with attention. Indeed, in one's mind, the past is defined as much by how you interact with it now as it is by what happened. It is an entity you can create a relationship with. Much like a love affair, the richness of the relationship stems from the effort put into creating more raw material for the future—things that will someday fill the treasure chest—and then honoring the past, a truth many people resist with love and resist with time too. We are always tempted to overindulge the experiencing self—the present—at the expense of other versions of ourselves. But here, especially, time discipline leads to time freedom. We say that "we want more time," said NYU psychology professor Lila Davachi in the talk she gave at the TEDWomen conference in 2016, but "what we really want is more memories."

The creation of these memories is within our control when

life is oriented toward adventure. It is easier not to choose adventures of both physical and emotional varieties. It is easier not to curate them afterward. It takes time to do more with memory than shoving old receipts into books or accidentally catching a whiff of honeysuckle, but doing so stretches time. This wooing of memory creates a deeper sense of self. The future is compelling. The past is rich. This mind-set is crucial to feeling like you have all the time in the world.

How the Brain Remembers

That more memories means more time may not seem immediately apparent. Understanding this connection requires knowing how the brain processes and archives what is going on around it. We have short-term, active engagement with the immediate world. We can repeat back a phone number and remember putting the coffee mug in the microwave (usually). But a lot of what passes through our existence is either archived deep in something akin to a reference library's stacks or tossed in the trash entirely.

An example: Do you have any recollection of today's date, two years ago? Maybe if you just started a new job you do, or if you had some noteworthy success or failure.

Most likely, though, there was nothing that made that day stand out from others. The routine was comfortable enough in the moment. On a day just like this, you got up, got yourself and possibly other people ready, commuted to work, answered emails, attended meetings, went home, made dinner, watched TV, and went to bed, but routines are comfortable for a reason. We don't have to think about them. Thinking and cataloging consume energy. If there is nothing to think about, there is no reason to catalog any of it. This is the brain deciding, with reason, that life would be unlivable if we remembered all 15.5 to 17.5 waking hours of every day. Some aspects of life are utilitarian. Your brain does not need to remember getting dressed this morning. Wise people often structure their lives to limit the brain space devoted to utilitarian concerns. A curated wardrobe of eleven flattering work outfits preserves cognitive capacity for difficult decisions.

It makes sense, but when it comes to time and memory, here is how this plays out. The brain decides that if you drive the same one-hour route to work 235 mornings a year, and you do so for the roughly 4.25 years that compose the average job tenure, these one thousand trips can be telescoped in memory into one trip.

Just like that, one thousand hours becomes one hour. That two-hour Tuesday-morning status meeting that always has you watching the clock? Each one seems endless, but they are similarly endless, and so in hindsight shrink to nothing. The usual weeknight routine of scrolling through headlines before bed consumes hours, but they are forgettable hours.

When enough sameness like this stacks up, whole years disappear into memory sinkholes. At a rate of one thousand hours becoming one hour, an 800,000-hour life would become like eight hundred hours: the equivalent of less than five weeks. As philosopher and psychologist William James writes on time, "Emptiness, monotony, familiarity, make it shrivel up." Time is measured only in the changing heights of children: "I can't believe how much you've grown!" This is said in astonishment to a child you saw three years ago, which did not fill the cognitive space of 26,280 hours.

Some of this is inevitable, and yet, contrasted with adult routine, other parts of life seem more expansive. Ask around and you'll find that almost everyone believes time moves faster now (when we are older) than in the past (when we were younger). Time itself plods along at the same pace, so the only way to explain this seeming acceleration is that our perception changes.

James touts this explanation: When we are young, life is the opposite of those thousand identical commutes. All is new. And not only are we seeing things for the first time, we're figuring life out, and thus taking risks we might not take as an adult. This creates emotional intensity that likewise deepens time.

There is something to this. I see this in the different ways my children and I interact with time and the physical world. One snowy January day a few years ago, I followed Sam, then six, into the backyard to keep an eye on him. We trudged through untouched snow that came up to my knees and close to his waist. He followed behind me until we came to a small tree. Then he broke off to labor across the drifts, climbed the tree, and inched out along a limb that was perhaps six feet in the air. He talked to himself softly for a long time. I strained to listen. Eventually I realized he was working up the courage to leap off the branch and into the snow. In those moments there was fear, and daring, and finally exhilaration as he threw himself into the powdery white. Mix this intensity with the novel, nearly unrecognizable landscape, and his brain was laying tracks of the sort my boots were cutting through the snow. My brain—stuck on more pedestrian matters, such as whether my 12:30 P.M. phone call was happening despite schools and many offices being closed—was more of a well-shoveled, well-trod driveway. It would not have occurred to me to leap off a branch, even subtracting any grown-up fear of injury.

Why Is Today Different?

The memories that do stand out in adulthood tend to show this newness or intensity. There are the big ones. I can recall my first few dates—literally, the dates on the calendar—with my husband in extensive detail. I can remember the births of my children, particularly the fourth, whose swift arrival necessitated a frantic drive to the hospital. Pain slows the experience of time, and I remember every excruciating traffic light between the house and the hospital parking lot. Indeed, my mind drifts to that night every time I stop at those traffic lights now.

Such experiences are by their nature memorable. So are vacations with their novelty. As Davachi explained in her talk, if you think of each discrete event that happens to you as a memory unit, "in an environment with a lot of variety and change, you're forming far more memory units than in an environment with very little change. It's these units—the number of these units—that determine our estimates of time later on. More units, more to remember, and time expands."

Going through normal life, you might only remember half a dozen interesting events over the past two weeks. Travel somewhere exotic, and you can have half a dozen new experiences before breakfast. Your brain has no idea what it will need in the future, so it is marking all of it. That can make a day feel like a fortnight. A similar phenomenon could happen on a day that featured half a dozen emotionally intense situations.

I know I have experienced this. The week I heard Lila Davachi speak about time and memory featured both novelty and intensity. So it is scored—by date—into my mind. I spent a long weekend before (October 21–24, 2016) at Disney World and Universal Studios in Orlando, Florida. We stayed late at the parks, after the crowds had left, and rode Harry Potter and the Forbidden Journey through the Dementors and past dragons. We sped along on Epcot's Test Track through the Florida night. Amusement park rides are designed to be novel and intense. That is their whole purpose, and they did not disappoint.

Home on Monday the twenty-fourth, I flew on Tuesday the twenty-fifth to San Francisco, where I ran along the Embarcadero early that first morning of the twenty-sixth, taking in the gorgeous bay and the caws of the birds. I did a test run of my TED Talk, and met my fellow speakers. I practiced again and again in my hotel room. The next morning, Thursday the twenty-seventh, I did my hair and let the makeup artist press on my fake lashes. I remember standing behind the stage curtains and doing those power poses that Amy Cuddy recommended for confidence in her TED Talk. I took the TED stage. With the lights on me, I spoke for my twelve minutes. The audience laughed when they were supposed to laugh, and nodded when they needed to, and though those twelve minutes are the same length of time that it takes me to make my children chocolate-chip pancakes in the morning, I know that I am more likely to think of this experience when I remember 2016 than any given morning making breakfast.

I was fortunate enough to speak in the first session of the conference, so I could relax for the others. Even so, time didn't speed up. I listened to dozens of other speakers create memorable experiences in their twelve to eighteen minutes. Many talks were intense, on topics from sexual assault to the murder of one speaker's family. As I sat in the hotel bar that Friday afternoon, waiting to go to the airport for my red-eye home, I could not believe that I had arrived in Orlando a mere 168 hours before. I had just lived through one of the longest weeks of my life.

Not all weeks can be like that. I don't want all weeks to be like that. I barely saw my youngest child (it was a big-kids-only trip to Orlando), and I did precious little writing. Leaving aside the practical matter of earning a living, I am genuinely happy puttering with my words, even if no given session of parking myself in my chair stands out from the rest.

There is nothing wrong with routines. People draw pleasure and comfort from routines, and good routines in the long run make success possible. It is partly the contrast between normal life and the heightened experience of travel that makes vacations memorable. In the absence of any normality, novelty itself would become tiring.

What I am arguing for is not the absence of routine, or that you need to figure out one thousand different ways to commute during those one thousand otherwise identical mornings. It is for a different balance between the normal and the novel than people might naturally create. I believe that even normal days can be made special—can be made *memorable*—with a mind-set toward adventure. I believe that consciously choosing to create such memories will stretch the experience of time.

In the Jewish tradition, before the Passover meal, the youngest person at the table asks, "Why is this night different from all other nights?" In the Passover context the answer is that the night celebrates a defining event in extended family history, but this is a wonderful question in a secular context too. One might inquire this of any twenty-four hours. *Why is today different from all other days?* Why should my brain bother holding on to the existence of this day as it curates the museum of my memories?

I would venture that for nine out of ten days, and maybe for a higher proportion, most of us have no answer. The day is forgettable. So it is forgotten. When the ratio of forgotten days climbs high enough, that is a shame. Not all days can be Passover (or any holiday you celebrate), but that doesn't mean there can be nothing setting the day apart, or maybe just one day of every handful apart, hallowing it in the treasure chest.

Dorie Clark, a personal branding guru and author of *Stand Out* and *Entrepreneurial You,* has spent much of the past few years happily building her business, but when she came to the end of 2015, she "had this alarming realization," she says. "People asked me the question 'What do you like to do besides work?' and I didn't have any kind of answer for them. Work was all I did, and I realized that was upsetting." It was upsetting philosophically—there is more to life—but it also felt financially foolish. "I live in New York City. If all I was doing was working, I could do that from anywhere. I could do that from a shack in the middle of the desert," she says. "Why pay to live in one of the world's most expensive cities if I wasn't taking advantage of it?"

So in 2016 she came up with an idea of having at least one uniquely New York adventure each week. "That way, I would feel at the end of the year like I'd taken advantage of the place where I was living."

She attacked her goal with gusto. "I get motivated by quantifying things, so I started writing everything down. Whenever I did something it went into my phone." Soon, the list included a tour of Hasidic Brooklyn and a visit to the Armory. She checked out the Lower East Side Tenement Museum and the Gansevoort Market. She took in an Upright Citizens Brigade comedy show, and saw a Samantha Bee taping. She even got to see Jerry Seinfeld perform when he stopped by a comedy club (unannounced!) where she'd gone for an evening's entertainment. She went to Broadway shows and ate at Sardi's. She biked the path along the West Side Highway. She hit the Russian Tea Room, the Rainbow Room, and the Tribeca Film Festival, and ate her way through a list of the city's best pizzerias. She visited a shopping mall in Queens at the far end of the 7 line in Flushing, where the vast food court features more than thirty stalls selling authentic Asian cuisine. The project created its own momentum. By January 2017, she had documented far more than fifty-two only-in-New-York memories.

The goal encouraged several positive behaviors. First, she became more mindful of choosing how she would spend her free time. While New York adventures can just happen, her weekly target meant that she "was making an effort to seek them out." She became a subscriber of *Time Out New York* because, she says, "I needed that information to inform my choices." In the past, she used to read about things and "maybe save the article, and say this would be nice to do someday." To a busy person, "someday" is a synonym for "never." Thanks to her list, "someday" became a specific day on the calendar. The goal also helped her choose between activities such as a movie or a museum exhibit. Without the New York–specific criteria, "I might otherwise not have a good reason to decide between those things. But I could see a movie anywhere or anytime. I can't go to this time-limited museum exhibit in New York [anywhere or anytime], so I should privilege that."

Forcing herself to venture out of the apartment and into new neighborhoods means that "now New York itself is this rich landscape of memories and associations where it wasn't necessarily before." Even walking from the subway conjures up stories: *I did this. Remember when we did that?* A Saturday night when you see Jerry Seinfeld certainly answers the question of how today is different from all other days. In a city like New York, some of this is pricey, which I suppose is the usual reason for choosing Netflix over the Brooklyn Museum, but much is free. I well remember the early morning from my New York years when I traveled downtown to see the old Fulton Fish Market, with the mountains of ice, the fires where vendors burned their crates, the bloody mess of fish heads glistening and pungent in the dark under the highway.

Shockingly Interesting Lives

Even daily life can answer the question of difference. In my time-perception survey, people who agreed that "Yesterday, I did something memorable or out of the ordinary with my time" were 14 percent more likely than average to agree that they generally had enough time for the things they wanted to do.

I analyzed the time logs from the thirty people with the highest time-perception scores, and found that their lives were shockingly interesting for a March Monday. One woman bought movie tickets online at 6:00 P.M. and by 7:00 P.M. was in the theater, viewing *Beauty and the Beast* with her family. One respondent picked up a friend and went to a community event for social entrepreneurs. Another fixed dinner for her ten-year-old at 7:00 P.M., and then hit a local spa for a massage at 8:00 P.M. I spotted a 9:00 P.M. salsa dancing session on one log. One Los Angeles respondent and her cousin entertained various children by having them try on an actor family member's bird costume, resulting in much hilarity. One respondent ushered the babysitter in at 8:00 P.M. and promptly zipped off to a big-band concert. Remember, this was on a *Monday night*.

Even people without such obvious adventures were still likely to spend their evening hours doing something more interesting than watching TV: a family trip to the park, for instance, to take advantage of late March's longer light, or a postprandial 8:00 P.M. stroll.

What is memorable? What creates emotional intensity? Bits of time can become bits of joy. For instance:

- If you like to be a regular somewhere for lunch, and there is much pleasure in being one, maybe you go there two or three times per week and try somewhere else the other days.

- Park in a different lot some ordinary Tuesday and take a morning walk through a new neighborhood. Then make an evening stop in a store that intrigued you when you passed it on the way into work.

- Seek out a colleague you've previously only said hello to for a real conversation.

- Speak up in a meeting you normally just observe.

- Write a letter to the editor for the local paper some night when you would have watched TV, and enjoy your sense of pride and accomplishment when you see it printed three days later.

- On a summer night, hit the neighborhood pool for an evening swim.

- Put a picnic blanket in the backyard and eat breakfast outside.

- Slip out of work early on a Wednesday and meet your spouse for a drink before taking your normal train home.

- Invite friends to join you for a short hike in a nearby state park—you know, the one with the gorgeous pine trees, the one you've lived near for the past four years and have yet to visit.

Three Versions of the Self

It is simple enough to make a day different, and therefore memorable. This raises the question of why we don't do it, or at least why fewer people bother than would enjoy the memories afterward. The answer is that the "self" is really multiple selves:

- The anticipating self is wondering about, planning, and worrying about the future.

- The experiencing self is in the here and now.

- The remembering self thinks back to the past.

Creating more memories—and hence creating more time—requires privileging the anticipating and the remembering selves above the experiencing self in ways that require serious self-discipline.

One small concession in this difficult project is that when it comes to pleasurable adventures, the anticipating self and the remembering self are often aligned. Indeed, reports Davachi, "They involve the same brain systems." To anticipate an event or to remember an event, your brain constructs a narrative out of familiar images for something that isn't happening now. It doesn't matter that the events actually happened in the past or are only in your mental picture of what might happen in the future. Notes Davachi: "The brain doesn't respect time."

The anticipating self is the planner who sets anchors in the future. As I picture this version of myself, I see her watching that documentary about the Galápagos Islands, and looking at her vacation schedule and figuring out when she might be able to go there. The anticipating self hears from a friend about the amazing exhibit at the local art museum and sees that Friday evening might be a great time to go. Once she sets her intentions, she mulls over these plans, thinking about what these future experiences will be like. When the anchors are strong enough, the anticipating self can pull the experiencing self into the future when she needs to. Many a dreary March commute has been warmed by the sun at the beach rental, booked for July. Indeed, anticipation may account for most of the happiness associated with events. Knowing you have a reservation for your favorite restaurant on Saturday night allows you to experience some of the pleasure you'd have in the moment of eating. Unlike the moment of eating, however, anticipated pleasure can extend for *weeks*.

The remembering self is anticipation's sidekick. She (or he—depending on your gender) is the keeper of your identity. She smiles at the photo of her children, on the desk, from when they were small and the family spent that spring Saturday at the botanical gardens. All is color and happiness and the baby's fat fingers clutching at that young mother's neck. Memorialized like this, the day can hold its own in the wash of the past. It can be recalled and referred to, setting a marker in the current of time.

We can anticipate for years. We can remember for decades. The challenge is that the present—the moment occupied by the experiencing self—has a disproportionate effect on our actions, given its fleeting nature. The remembering self loves that photo of the children in the garden, but that's easy for her to say. Bliss is possible in the past and in the future but seldom in the present. To get the children to the botanical gardens, the experiencing self had to deal with the four-year-old's bitter complaints that he doesn't want to go anywhere, the two-year-old's diaper blowout on the way out the door, and the baby screaming and throwing her pacifier somewhere in the car. It is all such bother. The anticipating self thought it would be fun to go to the art museum on a Friday night—when admission is free and there's a bar and music!—and the remembering self will fondly recall the masterpieces, and maybe even a new friend made in line for chardonnay, but the experiencing self is tired after work. The experiencing self is the one who will have to brave the cold and the rain and the Friday-night traffic.

The experiencing self resents this division of labor. So she throws a tantrum. She ignores the anticipating and remembering self and justifies her betrayal with statements that are certainly true: *I'm tired.* The museum will be there next Friday. So I'll just watch TV. Immediate effortless pleasure wins out over the more effortful variety. Writes philosopher Robert Grudin in *Time and the Art of Living,* "We pamper the present like a spoiled child." We indulge its whim to scroll through Facebook posts from people we never liked in high school anyway. Then this time is nothing. It disappears as if it doesn't exist.

How to Keep the Experiencing Self's Tyrannies in Check

There is no easy answer for solving this past-present-future dilemma. People are horrible at considering their future selves. That's one reason people underinvest for retirement. But I do think that knowing this aspect of human nature helps. When

I catch myself listening too much to the experiencing self (*You know, the kids are happy watching TV and if you get in the car for forty-five minutes after drinking coffee you'll really need to find a bathroom at the end of the trip and . . .*), I pause and try to re-member that this is just one actor carrying on a monologue in what should be a three-actor play. Then I repeat a two-part mantra:

- Plan it in.

- Do it anyway.

If my anticipating self wanted to do something, my remem-bering self will be glad to have done it. Indeed, my experiencing self may even enjoy parts of it. I am tired now, but I will always be tired, and we draw energy from meaningful things.

I also remember this: all time passes. Whether I do anything today or not, eventually I will be on the other side of the next twenty-four hours. It can be filled with "nothing" (in this case, meaningless somethings), or it can be filled with something more intriguing. As for that intriguing something, even if my anticipating self is more timid, eventually I will be on the other side of this activity. If it doesn't kill me—and most things won't—I'll be left with a good story. I can push.

And so I do. One December Saturday not long ago, I had hemmed and hawed about doing everything that might conceiv-ably fit in the day. The forecast called for snow, and the day's proposed itinerary involved breakfast with Santa at Longwood Gardens, and then a wrestling meet for Sam, and a train trip into NYC with him to meet the other kids and my husband—who wanted to go to the American Museum of Natural History—and a quick stop at a holiday party my husband wanted to attend. Then I would go downtown solo to take in a choir concert. I would take the train back to Trenton to get my car, and drive home after midnight.

It was a hard day. Leave aside the logistics of handing off children in Midtown Manhattan, or that my toddler began throwing food in my husband's colleague's apartment. The drive home was what had me completely stressed out, because fog had rolled in so thick that I could not see which entrance to the Pennsylvania Turnpike from U.S. 1 went east or west. Only my familiarity with the toll plaza steered me straight. Yet once I woke the next morning and had my coffee, what lingered of the day was mostly seeing my kids on Santa's lap, the bloodred poinsettias in the snow-covered greenhouse, the moment the referee hoisted my little wrestler's arm up in victory, and a gorgeous wash of voices singing of warmth, wonder, and birth.

Notes Dorie Clark: "We're making choices regardless, by dint of how we spend our time. So do you want to make the choices consciously or unconsciously?"

Conscious fun takes effort. This seeming paradox—*Why should fun be work?*—stops us in our tracks. So we overindulge in effortless fun (scrolling through Instagram posts about dinner parties), and underindulge in effortful fun (throwing a dinner party ourselves). But "although minutes spent in boredom or anxiety pass slowly," writes Grudin, "they nonetheless add up to years which are void of memory."

It is the effortful fun that makes today different, and makes today land in memory. You don't say "Where did the time go?" when you remember where the time went.

Woo Your Memories

But planning in fun, and doing it regardless, is not the whole story for stretching time. Memory must be cultivated. Having a real relationship with memory requires treating it as a living thing. In a way, it is. Things do not just happen, the mind recording them exactly as they happened, with these memories accessible as one might look up a number in the phone book. The mind chooses to remember some things more vividly than others. It constructs stories from disparate events, or at least its impressions of disparate events—which may not be how others saw the same events—which then become the tighter truth to you the more you tell the story. Try asking spouses, separately, to describe their wedding. They were both there. It definitely happened, but both will remember different things. They will recount the day in different ways.

Some memories will score deep regardless of your desires. That's why I remember the traffic lights en route to the hospital.

In most cases, though, you can help the process along. You can actively choose to document your adventures in ways that will help you pull them out.

Modern sorts need no encouragement to take photos. What we do need encouragement for is their active curation: choosing the best to make photo books that we will pause from our days to ponder rather than just having a big file on the iPhone that will be lost when the iPhone gets forgotten on the bus. There are many reasons to keep a journal; nudging the day's events into active memory is one. My time logs document in detail how I spent past days. Scrapbooks elevate the fine art of memory keeping.

Cementing memories can be a social thing too. At the dinner table, ask people to tell stories of their days. Consciously set memories into your senses; even a bar of hotel soap can become associated with a trip if you make a point of sniffing it daily during your vacation.

That helps in the future. The trouble is that we haven't necessarily done this with previous experiences. But as Grudin writes, "Experience merely forgotten is seldom beyond recall, if we try hard and patiently to bring it back. It is only when we forget having forgotten that a door closes between us and the past."

Research supports this poetic notion that memories can become sharper after the fact, even if the research is generally in the context of negative memories.

Davachi reports that she and her colleagues conducted a

study on this aspect of memory, with two phases. In phase one, people were shown neutral images (animals, tools). In the second phase, they were shown similar images (animals, tools) and given a light shock on the wrist when one of the kinds of images (only animals or only tools) appeared. Not surprisingly, subjects developed sharper memories of whatever kind of image came with a shock in phase two. People shocked when they saw tools remembered the tools better than they remembered the animals. Curiously enough, though, they also eventually had better recall of these kinds of images from phase one—*before* they were shocked. The shocks taught their brains that one particular category of images was important, and so their brains searched back through the past for examples, and gave these examples new places of prominence.

Most of us don't want to shock ourselves to sharpen memories, but this research does suggest that we can do things in the present to deepen our experience of the past. I like the image of wooing memory. Perhaps it's exposing ourselves to certain songs, sights, or smells. Proust's fragrant madeleine conjured up more than seems proper for a mere cookie. "Similarly, when we strive to reconstruct some period deep in our past," writes Grudin, "it is helpful to search for some physical detail which is remembered almost viscerally and which, when felt again, may bring with it the whole emotional context of earlier time."

I recommend carving out time for "dwelling in the past," a phrase that has a more negative connotation than it deserves. On a long car trip, play those albums from a time you wish to remember. Songs can resurrect teenage elation and longing. You are suddenly seventeen, and in your car, and turning to that equally wide-eyed person next to you. You are pulling close for a kiss you can still remember twenty-five years later.

These days, I unearth memories like an archaeologist. How many more travel receipts, and the equivalent, are hidden around the house? I pause to look at a white coat in my closet. It is dingy now, but I cannot bring myself to dump it, because I touch its fuzzy sleeves and for a moment I am twenty-four, and wearing it on a weekend trip to London with the man who was four months away from asking me to marry him. I was in love, and dazzled that someone might whisk me to London for the weekend, and I was in that coat, and in the first pass of memory all is bliss, though I have no doubt I got off that plane as jet-lagged as I have ever been after a flight to Europe. That was the experiencing self, and as I think about it more, I remember other trials the experiencing self endured. The Heathrow Express was broken, so we took a cab (in traffic) downtown. The hotel magnanimously let us check in early, for what we later learned was the price of an extra night. My older and more well-traveled beau noted that in the developing world, cabdrivers would cheat you out of two dollars. It takes a fancy London hotel to stick you with a bill for an extra two hundred pounds. Yet in memory the white coat conjures up walking through an autumnal Hyde Park, and staring into each other's eyes over pints in a pub.

What Do You Get When You Cross Homecoming and Ache?

Cleaning out a desk or cleaning out a closet can unearth relics. Or sometimes, we can do bigger things to revisit certain times of our lives.

In May 2017, I celebrated my twentieth anniversary of graduating from the Indiana Academy for Science, Mathematics, and Humanities, a public residential high school for juniors and seniors, by returning to give the commencement address. The weight of years felt heavy; I knew that the seniors in the audience had not been born yet when I got my diploma. But despite my rational knowledge of this space, when I flew to Indianapolis that Friday, drove on I-69 through the cornfields to Muncie, Indiana, parked on those familiar streets and opened the car door, it was as if I had never left.

I breathed in the familiar smell: the trees, the White River. I remembered showing up there as a sixteen-year-old in 1995. I was eager to be out on my own. I wanted to learn everything I could. I sensed, then, that if I could do well on that stage I might be given more opportunities, ones that would take me out of those cornfields I was now flying back to in 2017.

The landscape of Ball State University, and the "Village" of stores nearby, quickly unlocked the map that still existed somewhere in my mental archives. Each building unearthed another memory. The old coffee shop was still there. It was under new management and sporting a different name, but looking much as it did. The White Rabbit used-book store was still in business. The familiar-looking proprietor was still not wearing shoes, even if twenty years later I looked trustworthy enough that he let me keep my bag as I perused the stacks. I am quite sure that much of the inventory had been on those shelves the last time I was there. I walked behind my old dorm and found the window from my junior-year bedroom. I remembered staring out that window every morning at the dining hall, the classrooms, the parking lot, the Dumpster.

I tried to remember what it was like to be that sixteen-year-old girl. I tried to remember what she thought, what she wondered about the future. Would she be happy with my life now? I would like to imagine so, though I suspect she harbored ambitions for her pulpy novels to be as ubiquitous as Nicholas Sparks in the White Rabbit. In any case, in the heat of that late May day I let myself dwell on a few memories that made me smile. Then I felt the tug of some harder moments too. It was never an easy place. The Greek roots of "nostalgia" combine the words for *homecoming* and *ache*. Such sweet pain is a complex emotion, but a beguiling one. It is why we turn the radio up for songs that can conjure such wistful intensity.

As I walked around the campus, I mulled this thought: dwelling in the past requires a forgiving mind-set. The emotional dramas that are long water under the bridge mattered to me once as I hunted through the stacks in the White Rabbit, as I gazed at that eternal Dumpster. They consumed my time once.

I should understand the person who cared so deeply. She is part of me. Whoever I am is because of what she learned. As I get to know her, the lived hours of my life become larger, no longer telescoped into little moments as I acknowledge them.

Onstage that Saturday, I stood in my 1997 cap and gown in front of the shiny faces. They were who I once was. At that moment, they had more time than memories. Soon I will have more memories than time—maybe I already do. I told them to make life memorable. Do something memorable daily, because that is the only way to keep time from slipping through our fingers. We fully live our hours; we know how we spent those hours. Then, looking back, as we honor their memory, we can know who we truly are.

THREE

DON'T FILL TIME

*An hour—why, there was no way of measuring the
length of an empty hour! It stretched away into infinity
like the endless road in a nightmare; it gaped before
her like the slippery sides of an abyss. Nervously she
began to wonder what she could do to fill it.*

—Edith Wharton, *Twilight Sleep*

don't recall how I found myself reading Ken Blanchard and
the late Spencer Johnson's *The New One Minute Manager* the
other day. Someone must have mailed me a copy when it came
out, and perhaps in a procrastination-induced decluttering fit,
I found it in my teetering book pile.

I think what most people take from this perennial bestseller
is that managers should catch employees doing something good.
Praise them and, magically enough, you get more of whatever
induced the praise.

But what stood out for me was the authors' description of
their master manager's schedule. A young man on a quest to

learn the secrets of management hears about a gentleman who possesses this wisdom. "Curious, he phoned the assistant to this special manager to see if he might get an appointment. To his surprise, the assistant put him through to the manager immediately." The young man asks when he might visit, assuming the manager will be swamped with all the great managerial stuff he is doing. The hook is that he isn't. "The manager said 'Anytime this week is fine, except Wednesday morning. You pick the time.'" This, of course, excites the reader to know why he is so free.

Or perhaps the better question is, *How?* To say this lightness bears no resemblance to the typical office worker's schedule is understating things. The more time logs I study, the more struck I am by how intertwined the concepts of "work" and "scheduled meeting" have become. Six to eight hours of meetings or conference calls per day is not unusual, particularly for senior people who have roles on multiple projects. It gets to the point where noncollaborative work must be done at night or on weekends. Open space for thinking? Not while you're on the clock.

Yet not everyone has a jammed schedule. I saw this when setting up an interview with Jeff Heath.

A connoisseur of time-management books—he introduced me to Robert Grudin's *Time and the Art of Living*—Heath began thinking about scheduling strategies in sixth grade. These days he's running Matrix Applied Technologies, a subsidiary of

Matrix Service Company, which makes and sells equipment for oil and petrochemical storage tanks. Based in Tulsa, Oklahoma, Heath is also responsible for a manufacturing facility just outside Seoul, South Korea, and a regional office in Sydney, Australia. This portfolio has him on the road about a third of the time, managing people across multiple time zones.

He responded to a query of mine about schedules, and after we exchanged emails I asked if we could set up a call. I assumed I would be offered a fifteen-minute window at 3:45 P.M. someday weeks hence. But as we looked toward the end of the week, he told me, "My calendar is pretty open right now, so why don't you let me know a couple times that work best for you."

It was the anytime-except-Wednesday-morning manager all over again. When we got on the phone, I had to ask him: How was it, there in corporate America, that anyone looking through his schedule could see daylight?

"It's more of a mind-set," he told me. "Do I have all the time in the world? Well, I've got the same amount of time as everyone else. I think it's how you approach time."

As we talked, I learned that Heath's approach to time was key to escaping the "busy" trap that frustrates so many people who want space for reflection but find their schedules clogged.

First, he truly believes that time is valuable. Plenty of people say they believe that, but not like this: Heath never gets on a fourteen-hour flight to Asia without a plan for the full fourteen hours. He thinks through when he should sleep, how much time he has to work, exactly what he should accomplish during that time, and when he will relax so he can manage his energy. I have been on enough planes to see that people who in other contexts would say they'd kill for an uninterrupted three hours—let alone fourteen—fritter away this time. They're flipping between TV shows, or paying for internet access, then loading up NYDailyNews.com and reading about a Brooklyn woman who killed her mother over a dispute about their pet cat. Even the "productive" sorts will spend these hours answering emails as they come in rather than tackling the focused work they could knock out under uninterrupted conditions.

Heath does the deep stuff. Then, because he's used his plane time, this lessens the pressure on the hours when he's not on a plane. He can stack the work that takes time but requires less focus into his purposefully long workdays in Australia and Asia. The goal is to be able to work less when he's with his family in Tulsa. As he calculated for me, working seventy-five hours a week when you're on the road a third of the time, and working thirty-five to forty hours a week when you're home, comes out to a respectable fifty-hour average.

But fundamentally, here's his secret: "I *like* white space on my calendar," he says. Despite the lamentations, most people do not. We privilege stuff on a schedule as evidence that we are doing something. Or as Heath puts it, "People like having meetings just because it makes them feel like they're busy, and useful, and productive." Anything that is put on a calendar for a certain time, and involves other people, will automatically rise up the hierarchy of importance over space, whether it deserves to or not.

This is good to know if you're trying to get yourself to the gym—schedule a meeting with your trainer at 7:00 A.M.!—but this facet of human nature has predictable consequences. Picture a couple trying to figure out which one of them will stay home to let in a plumber who needs to do an emergency repair on a broken pipe. The party that has three meetings scheduled for the morning is likely to claim a greater need to get to the office, even if the other would have spent those morning hours solving his or her most important business dilemmas. Someone who often has six hours of meetings a day might call a day with two meetings "light," though the unfilled hours could be spent doing consequential things.

If the bias is that you are supposed to look busy because a crowded schedule is evidence to the world of your importance, then there's always the temptation to fill time. The temptation is to allow things on the schedule because they might be interesting, or to say yes to things because you are available and someone asks. People ask to be cc'd on emails, and fret when they're not invited to meetings. They don't actually want to have hours of white space, which is why when such hours do occur people immediately pick up their phones and complain about their in-boxes.

Edith Wharton, that shrewd observer of humanity, satirized

this fear of space in her 1927 novel *Twilight Sleep*. Her bustling heroine, Pauline Manford, is forever flitting between appointments, cramming in newfound spiritual pursuits in the fifteen-minute slots between meetings with household employees and philanthropic committees. An empty hour made Manford "feel as if the world had rushed by and forgotten her," Wharton wrote. Such a terror that the world can (will!) continue without one's input "produced in her a sort of mental dizziness."

Heath does not subscribe to this philosophy. "If my calendar is wide open, that doesn't mean I don't have a lot to get done," he says.

It means seeing that a culture of managing through formal meetings has an opportunity cost. When everyone's in meetings all day, people wait to make decisions until they get to the appointed time on the calendar. That might be a long time from now, because everyone else has scheduled their formal meetings too. Heath would rather empower the smart people who work with him to make their own decisions based on clear objectives (which, incidentally, is what *The One Minute Manager* also suggests), and be available should anyone need to run something by him. Because Heath isn't in meetings all day, the people who report to him know they can always call or stop by. He's fine with such drop-in chats because he's taken the time while on planes to do the work that requires hours of uninterrupted focus.

Because he isn't in meetings all day, he has the mental space to deal with what employees bring to him. Even if they're bringing serious matters, it all fits—the dirty secret of meetings is that by their nature they consume more time than the matters often justify. They are always scheduled for thirty or sixty minutes, no matter how much needs to get done. They extract transaction costs; if someone has a 10:00 A.M. meeting, she's likely to stop doing any deeper work by about 9:45 A.M. After meetings, people cycle through their transition rituals: an email check, then a glance at favorite apps before going into anything deeper. This means that an hour-long meeting can easily consume the mental space of ninety minutes. If there's another meeting scheduled an hour later, less than thirty minutes will be available between them.

This then creates its own vicious cycle. People assume you're not doing any work besides meetings, so they schedule meetings to force deadlines. They call meetings to share information, because it's assumed you're not reading your email, because you have so many meetings, and much of your email is about scheduling meetings.

To break this cycle, you have to consciously push back against schedule clutter. "It's like water," Heath says. "It will find the openings if you let it. You've got to be really diligent about saying 'Not today.'" He will tell people that they don't need to meet. He will decline meeting requests when he sees that someone else can handle the matter. He models that it's OK to call people without a scheduled call, or to solve something in five minutes in the hallway rather than scheduling a thirty-minute meeting two days hence.

Perhaps it seems risky, but he's found a surprising upside to looking like he doesn't have an overwhelming amount to do. This lightness seems to invite people to offer him new projects. Indeed, the reason his parent company gave him his business lines around the globe after acquisitions is that *he looked like he had space to take them on.*

Anyone can pack a schedule. People who get a lot done choose not to fill time, both at work and at home. Says Heath: "It's what you say no to as much as what you say yes to."

When Nothing Is Better Than Something

This chapter is about freeing up space. We learned in the previous chapter that adventures make life memorable, and memories stretch time. The challenge is that we often think we have no time for salsa dancing on Monday night because life is already full of other things: a burgeoning in-box, or colleagues' (or family members') demands.

Or at least it appears to be full of other things. In reality, the future is blank.

When I open a new spreadsheet on Monday morning, this visual representation of the upcoming week consists of 336 empty thirty-minute cells. Eventually the log will be filled. Eventually I will be on the other side of the next 168 hours, but even if you believe that everyone's future deeds are already recorded somewhere, from the human perspective the future is best understood as probabilities.

There are odds—ranging from nearly impossible to nearly certain—that various events will happen. These probabilities are based on larger forces in the world, choices made in the past, obligations taken on, plans, desires, and biological needs.

All these fill time, but sometimes expectations become so ingrained in our assumptions of the future that we become puppets performing one act after the next, based on how some unseen puppeteer moves us. We don't question these assumptions, because they are familiar enough to feel like truth. We forget that the performance consisting of the next 168 hours is seldom inevitable—that is, based on 100 percent unchangeable odds. I cannot control what lands in my in-box. I *can* control whether I spend my entire Wednesday trying to meet some unspoken standard of timely replies, or whether I recognize that email is only going to expand to fill all available space and then decide I'd rather take a long lunch to wander around an exhibit at the art museum. Much can be pushed back on, or perhaps is self-inflicted. In one workshop, I witnessed an employee speak of how she kept her phone with her all the time in their 24/7 company, only to have her manager note that just because that manager sent an email at 9:00 P.M. didn't mean she needed a response then.

People who are good stewards of time are careful not to fill precious hours with what doesn't feel like the best use of those precious hours. They know that what looks like nothing can be a better choice than something. They know that open space invites opportunity in a way a cluttered calendar can't. These moments of nothing, chosen because time is precious, also have the paradoxical result of making time feel plentiful.

Perhaps the best metaphor for this mind-set is the evolution of that modern obsession, decluttering. Over the past two decades, TV shows and magazines have preached the joy of purging one's possessions. Then in 2014, Japanese decluttering expert Marie Kondo rocketed onto the scene with a more fundamentalist twist. Don't just chuck stuff you don't like, she writes in *The Life-Changing Magic of Tidying Up*. Keep only that which "sparks joy."

I confess that I have mixed feelings about this tidying fetish, as evidenced by the stacks of books in my office. Still, when it comes to schedules, there is great power in evaluating all claims on time from the blank-slate perspective. Forget sunk costs ("We've spent three weeks on this project; we can't kill it now!"). Forget saving bits of time here and there by cleaning your shower while you're in it, or soaking your pasta before you boil it, or other such tips that fill out the front-of-book section in magazines. What would it be like to have nothing on your schedule that did not "spark joy"?

On a practical level, it is unworkable. Even people who work for themselves, or who have steep quantities of cash, still have the metaphorical equivalent of paper towels and other non-joy-sparking miscellany in their lives. I don't like going to the dentist, but as long as my teeth are in my mouth I can't delegate it.

Still, it's an ideal. A bit of schedule bravery, and smart

choices over time, can open up all kinds of space for thinking, creating, and experiencing. These are better ways to spend time than filling it with things of no pleasure or consequence.

The One-Hour Gap

On that March Monday of my time-diary study, everyone had twenty-four hours to fill. Perhaps it is not surprising that people in the top 20 percent of time-perception scores spent fewer hours working than people in the bottom 20 percent. However, the difference wasn't as stark as you might imagine. The average person worked 8.3 hours. Those who felt like they had the least time worked 8.6 hours; those who felt like they had the most worked 7.6 hours.

Most of these workers in all perception camps put in a standard seven- to nine-hour workday. It is possible that the one-hour gap between the top and bottom could, by itself, alter a person's perception of time. But because 8.6 hours is hardly an extreme workday, and indeed isn't that much off the 8.3-hour average, I'm not sure that the obvious explanation—that people working crazy hours feel like they have less time—is the correct one.

Instead, after looking through logs and studying highly productive people, I think the equation goes in a different direction.

Within the range of normal hours, professionals experience

much choice in how they spend their time. As we saw in chapter 1, people with more abundant time-perception scores were likely to have thought through their days ahead of time. Such strategizing boosts efficiency; planning your toughest work for the time when you have the most energy means a task might take one hour instead of two. That would chop an hour off a workday right there.

Planning conscious breaks during the day could have the same effect. Going for a thirty-minute walk at lunch, for instance, will clear your head and enable focus for the rest of the afternoon. That means you won't get stuck staying late to complete something that has to be done by the end of the day that you haven't gotten to because your addled brain keeps reading the same email six times in a row.

My takeaway from the logs was that people with high time-perception scores worked fewer hours because they chose not to fill all available space. They *could* have filled this space; they simply elected not to.

I saw another example of this phenomenon when *Inc.* magazine asked me to study the schedules of eight high-profile founders for their April 2017 issue. These people kept track of their time on November 29, 2016, which was a Tuesday.

The normal narrative of entrepreneurial life celebrates round-the-clock work. Yet for the most part, these entrepreneurs worked reasonable hours. Alexis Ohanian, cofounder of Reddit, logged 4.5 hours of meetings and four hours of other work for a total of 8.5 hours. Eric Ryan, cofounder of Method and now CEO of supplements company Olly, worked eight hours. Cal Henderson, CTO of Slack, worked about seven hours.

For comparison, on November 29, 2016, my time log showed me working nine hours. There is no way that the demand for my time is higher than the demand for these people's time.

Time is a choice; work hours often have *nothing* to do with how much you could be doing.

Instead, these successful entrepreneurs were choosing not to fill all available space. This was particularly evident in Henderson's schedule. As befits someone who designs productivity software, he had clearly thought through his time. He walked to work while listening to audiobooks at 2x or 3x speed, a habit that he reported helped him get through seventy-plus books in 2016. I know that's the sort of productivity hack that people get excited about, but the more important strategies were on display during his workday. On meetings: "It's easy to let them fill the time." So he insisted on agendas. The videoconference system would display a ten-minute countdown so things ended in a timely fashion. And then there was this: "At 2:30, I take a break. I like a few breathers throughout the day—I find having a couple of half-hour breaks is much less stressful than having constant, back-to-back meetings." Even with these breaks, though, by getting what mattered accomplished, he was able to leave the office at 5:00 P.M. and spend the evening with his wife and two-year-old son.

Time discipline leads to time freedom. Henderson was disciplined enough not to fill time, and the result was effective management of a rapidly growing company, and enough time to listen to audiobooks, exercise, and enjoy his family.

I suspect the reality is not that people have to work long hours and then feel like they have no time. It is that some people want to be sure to have time for all the things they want to do, and so they naturally structure their work lives to get stuff done efficiently.

Looking at the time-perception survey, recall that many of those with the highest scores had adventures waiting in the evening. When you have arranged to visit a friend at 8:00 P.M., you will hack through your emails more judiciously during the day than if you know you can just throw hours at your in-box later. As one survey respondent put it, "If I'm busy doing things I like, I'm too busy to say yes when people ask me to do [things] I don't like to do." Imposing boundaries on your work life goes a long way toward actually having more free time. That may be easier for some people than for others, but if you have the skills and resources to be reading this book, my guess is that you are not powerless. It's your life. Be bold.

Still, cleaning up the calendar can help make that mind-set easier. Such decluttering requires smart tactics. Studying the time logs of those with the highest time-perception scores, and interviewing them, I found that these tactics fell into three categories of time liberation: declaring independence, creating time dividends, and getting over the fear of boredom that is behind so many wasted hours.

A Time Jubilee

If you feel like you keep getting busier as time goes by, under-standing this one particular truth about schedules can trans-form your life: few things are meant to continue in perpetuity. Yet we think more about starting projects than figuring out how they will end. The result is that much stacks up. Even if indi-vidual commitments seem wise on their own, the mass of them derails larger goals.

The solution? Declare a time amnesty, or perhaps a "jubilee," in honor of that every-fifty-years biblical occasion when debts were canceled. At the start of the year, or some other auspicious date, declare independence from everything beyond life main-tenance for you and any family members or pets who physically depend on you. As it takes a while to extricate yourself from some obligations, you can also declare a future amnesty. Every-thing winds down by some date three to six months from now. At that point, you can evaluate all claims on your time with a bias toward deciding what to keep rather than what to get rid of. In honor of Marie Kondo, we might say that you will "Kon-Mari" your calendar.

If you kept a time log after reading chapter 1, look over it from this perspective. What currently fills your time? With every activity ask this question: *What is my purpose here?* This sounds like a big question, the sort whose answer goes on a tombstone, but it can be a smaller question too. Cooking dinner

on weeknights: What is my purpose here? Sorting the mail from
10:30 P.M. to 11:00 P.M., despite being tired enough to fall over:
What is my purpose here? That Tuesday-morning meeting you
have led since time immemorial and that everyone keeps tromp-
ing to, marking the passage of another 168 hours by its existence: Why do we do this?

There need not be a profound purpose. We plant tulip bulbs
in October because we enjoy the flowers in April. That is a good
reason. In many cases, so is *I have always done this.* Traditions
have their own weight and comfort, but the goal is conscious
weight and comfort. If there is no reason that satisfies you, then
the activity may fall under the "toss" category, even if that little
voice in your head is telling you that "everybody" does it.

Time is a choice, with the understanding that you must deal
with the consequences of your choices. People with all the time
in the world know that there are few things anyone has to do.
Some have psychologically assured themselves of this in various
ways. Creating a financial cushion is one tactic. There is great
freedom in working because you want to and not because you
have to. This mental space often leads to better work.

Even in the absence of copious capital, though, a little real-
ism leads to this conclusion: We are all less important than we
think we are. Earth will keep spinning on its axis regardless of
how the vast majority of us spend our time.

Another thought: All things end. Eventually there will come
a Tuesday morning without that Tuesday-morning meeting,

and possibly before that a Tuesday morning when you are not leading it. The question is, *Just how many Tuesdays pass before that morning comes to be?*

With this forward-looking mind-set, you can free up incredible time by being careful with all future uses of the word "yes." One reason we overburden our future selves is that we view them as different people. Because of this, we think we're assigning future work to someone who won't mind it, or at least won't mind it as much as our spoiled experiencing selves mind saying "no." Sure, October me can do this. October me won't be busy! October me can *totally* take this on. But, absent an intervening jubilee, come October, life will be much the same as it is now, with a similar level of cordwood stacked into the calendar. Only now you will also have this other commitment that you were lukewarm about added to the pile.

A better question when asked to take on something in the future: *Would I do this tomorrow?*

Of course not, you protest; you are busy tomorrow. You are booked solid! It is understandable that you couldn't actually do something tomorrow, but would you be tempted? Would you try to move things around to fit in this new opportunity?

If so, you'll be just as excited in October. If not, then maybe the answer is no.

You can also build in space with a calendar triage. On Friday afternoons, when planning the following week, look at what everyone has stuck on your calendar, or what you once thought would be a good idea. See what you can jettison. The answer might be more than you think. If you don't believe an obligation is worth an hour of the time you have left on the planet, or you feel unhappy about chopping up an otherwise open block of space, then maybe you should cancel the obligation, knowing it is best to do so ahead of time so everyone can make other plans.

You might minimize things you can't kill. You can see on your calendar that you're meeting with the same people on Tuesday and Thursday about different topics, but if you're disciplined at the first meeting, you could get through both agendas. That's straightforward enough, but when people get busy, they don't even look at what's coming up. They just shuffle from one meeting to the next like middle schoolers changing classes, figuring they'll deal with all needs as they come along. But then it's Thursday and you're staring at the same people from Tuesday and kicking yourself about this time—when it's a beautiful spring day, and you could have left work early to go for a run—burned in a beige conference room.

Even if you can't get rid of things or shorten them, you can minimize their mental cost with creative scheduling. It's hard to use small gaps of time between events well. Rather than scheduling meetings at 9:00 A.M., 11:00 A.M., and 1:00 P.M., you might be better off pushing all these meetings and phone calls into one window of 1:00 P.M. to 4:00 P.M. (with some space in between them to avoid running late), and then having 8:00 A.M. to 1:00 P.M. open to deploy as you wish. On weekends, you might do the same thing, compressing chores or errands into Saturday morning so the rest of the weekend is open.

Change Your Story

As you declare schedule independence, question everything. People tell themselves many stories about what is required in life. Such prattle:

- I'll *never* replace the income if I let go of this annoying freelance gig.

- I'll lose my job if I don't look busy when my boss walks in; I'd better be at my desk before she gets here in the morning.

- *No one* here takes a lunch break, so I can't.

- *Everyone* knows you can't start a successful business unless you work seventy hours per week.

Many of these stories fall apart under cross-examination. Unless you are physically chained to your desk, you can probably walk outside for some fresh air. You can go to bed if you're tired, even if the house is a mess. You do not have to bathe your kids nightly. You can delegate or outsource vast quantities of things. You can stop doing time-consuming tasks such as putting other people's clothing neatly in their drawers, or creating a department newsletter, and see what happens. It might be an educational experience for all involved!

By that I mean an educational experience for *you* because, curiously enough, the most common reaction other people will have to your shedding an obligation is *nothing*.

Everyone lives in his or her own little world. Many of us have convinced ourselves that people notice a lot more than they do. In reality, your boss is too busy to count how many employees are at their desks when she walks in the door. She is too worried about pleasing her own boss to notice if a dependable employee takes thirty minutes for lunch or forty-five. Most clients are not counting the hours between when an email is sent and when you respond. Indeed, I have sent replies after what I thought was an uncomfortably long time only to get back an answer with the phrase "Thank you for your swift response!" Your family may not notice most of the things you do for them. A father recently told me that he was doing the laundry on his usual schedule when he saw that his eleven-year-old son's contribution to the pile was unusually light. He went to check if there were dirty socks and underwear hidden somewhere. There weren't, because, as parents of preteen boys may have guessed, the child had not changed these items in days. Clearly, prompt laundry service wasn't high on his list of concerns.

That said, when you stop doing things, you might experience some pushback. Declaring independence at work and at home isn't easy, or everyone would do it. Spring cleaning a calendar takes elbow grease. If someone protests your time jubilee, treat it as a negotiation. Ask the aggrieved person to make a counter-offer. If it's a good one, feel free to take it, but if you find yourself looking at your life and realizing you'd pay good money to get something off your plate, that's a sign that it needs to go, whether its chucking involves paying good money or not.

I am always impressed when people declare time amnesties simply because they decide time is precious. Realistically, though, big changes in circumstance often force the issue.

Damon Brown, an author, speaker, and entrepreneur, became a father for the first time in 2013. His wife had a traditional job with health insurance, and with the couple wanting to have one parent mostly at home, Brown elected to take that role. In theory, this would require scaling down his professional ambitions—I know, as a self-employed parent, that it is hard to work without childcare—but as luck would have it, the universe delivered several opportunities to Brown around this time. He wanted to take them. So he squeezed in work during the baby's nap time. He worked when his wife could be home. And within the fifteen hours he chose to work each week, he became ruthless about deciding what was worth doing. He wrote his non-baby-related goals for any given day on one side of an index card. The goals that didn't fit onto the card weren't going to happen, so he needed to revise the list until it included only the most important things.

He kept doing this. "Suddenly, after several months, I realize I'm actually being productive!" he says. "The things that didn't get done weren't crucial." He no longer had space for them, so they had to go. Writing his short lists helped make clear that "all the stuff I have to do is not that overwhelming. If it is over-whelming, I know I'm doing too much stuff." Three important things a day is fifteen important things per week. Over a year, that's 750 important things.

And indeed Brown did a lot. He gave a TED Talk. He started two businesses, and saw one (an app called Cuddlr that was a media sensation for a bit) acquired. The experience taught him this: "How much time we actually have is less relevant than how we perceive it."

I don't recommend cutting your workweek down to fifteen hours, or the four hours some people think is possible. But even within a forty- to fifty-hour workweek, scheduling only fifteen hours of obligations might have some upsides. As with Jeff Heath, you might find that your organization offers you new opportuni-ties precisely because you do not look overscheduled.

I am not sure the exact mechanism by which this works. It may be that when you feel relaxed about your schedule, people notice that you seem calm and in control, and they want to work with you. It may be that you have longer conversations with more varied people when you are not rushing to get to the next thing. Those conversations lead to new projects that wouldn't have happened otherwise.

In any case, if you look like you cannot take on anything else, you probably won't be given anything else. But the burdens of your current schedule might be keeping you from seeking out greater things. In this sense, your busyness isn't productive. It's counterproductive.

Calling something "work" doesn't make it a more noble use of time than anything else. Work that doesn't advance you toward the life you want is still wasted time. You will never get those hours back, and we only get so many. Wrote Shakespeare in *Richard II,* "I wasted time, and now doth time waste me." Questioning the story that anything labeled as "work" is automatically important is the swiftest way to achieve time freedom.

Time Dividends

Brown calls the past four years of index card prioritization "easily the most productive of my life." Yet there is nuance to this point. One reason he was able to work fifteen hours per week after his son arrived is that he had been working fifty hours a week before. He had spent these hours developing his skills and network. "I have been doing my most basic work for a quarter of a century, so I know exactly how much material and resources I need," he says, "just as a veteran craftsman knows the correct amount of wood and nails to build a table." Such knowledge accrues bit by bit. The brain develops muscle memory, which makes much of what would have required deliberation mindless. Experience "makes it easier to manage your time and your energy."

Brown's insight is this: certain things we do in the present can open up space in the future. These investments of time pay off again and again, much like a stock can pay an annual dividend. People who seem to have lots of time have often structured their lives to create time dividends; as money dividends make a person rich, so time dividends make you feel like this resource is abundant.

These time dividends take many forms. One of the most life changing: hiring and training a good assistant. Next thing you know you're coming home from vacation not to an overloaded in-box but to one email, from your assistant, outlining what you missed, which isn't much, because he dealt with everything in your absence.

Becoming known as an expert in a field can create similarly huge dividends; researching and writing that white paper takes time, but having potential clients download it and then call you is much more efficient than you having to find potential clients and pitch your work to them.

It takes initiative to outfit a home office and ask to work there occasionally, but getting to skip the commute once or twice a week can open up space for all kinds of other things.

If you get a lot of emails from people seeking to "pick your brain," you could spend an hour creating a list of answers to frequently asked questions about your industry. Then, when someone emails asking for advice, you send the FAQ list, and invite them to send you back any follow-up questions. (Fun fact: most won't bother! But those who do are probably worth meeting and mentoring.)

Royce Phillips, who works in the commercial insurance industry, tells me that he spent years in a sales position requiring extensive travel (123 nights in 2015). When he visited a city, he would always set his meetings for the same times: 9:00 A.M., 10:30 A.M., lunch, 1:30 P.M., and 3:00 P.M. "People knew when they traveled with me that was going to be the schedule," he says, and so he could spend his time preparing for his meetings rather than trying to remember if today was the day with a 9:30 meeting and a 11:45 meeting, or if that was tomorrow, or the day after that.

You can create dividends on the home front too. Many wise parents have discovered the genius of teaching preteen and teenage children to cook simple recipes. It takes time up front to train them, and remind them to put ingredients on the grocery list, but the payoff could be years in which you don't have to cook on Monday or Tuesday nights.

Even minor wins add up. A runner who invests time in doing speed work might be able to change her comfortable pace from eleven minutes per mile to ten minutes. In a twenty-five-mile week, that frees up twenty-five minutes for stretching or strength training.

Designating a spot for keys, sunglasses, cell phone chargers, and public-transport passes, and then taking the extra second to make sure everything gets deposited in the right place, can remove the ten minutes of frantic hunting that makes people late in the morning.

To start building this capacity into your life, study how you spend your time. When you do an activity, ask yourself two questions:

- Will I ever do this again?

- If so, is there some system I could develop or something I could do now that would make future instances faster or easier?

The good news is that some of these time dividends naturally happen as you do things repeatedly and get better at them—just as Damon Brown describes. When he was first writing for business publications, any given article would require figuring out the right people to call, and hoping they'd get back to him, and then asking lots of questions, and not being able to use all the material. Pieces might go through many drafts as he figured out the right angle. Years in, he knows how to reach the right sources, and far less lands on the cutting-room floor. Speeches, likewise, take a long time to write and memorize. But as Brown has built his speaking career, he's been able to reuse material.

Sometimes life forces us to recognize and cash in these dividends, as Brown's drastically reduced workweek did. But often it's more nebulous. Even if you "save" time in one category of life, it's easy not to notice that saved time. It's easy to spend it mindlessly. So if you want to feel like you have more time, don't just structure your life to create time dividends. Notice these dividends that occur because of your decisions or systems you've built. Celebrate them. Drink a toast to their existence.

I am reminded to do this every two years or so when I register another child for school. When we moved to suburban Pennsylvania, one of the major upsides was being able to send our kids to an excellent public elementary school located a mile from our house. There were no worries about lotteries, wait lists, admissions tests, or private school applications. In early 2012, I visited the district headquarters. I produced my eldest son's birth certificate, his immunization record, and my property tax bill. I repeated this process in 2015 and 2017, and barring unforeseen developments, I will do so again in 2020. It takes about one hour, total, including my time in the car to get there. Friends who've applied to private schools speak of the process as feeling like a part-time job for several months, to say nothing of the time required to earn the money to pay tuition. I have never taken the rest of the week off after enrolling my children, but I could, and I would still be ahead.

Get Off Your Phone Already

All sorts of things can fill time if we let them: busywork, inefficiencies. But I truly believe the worst time-filling culprit is our own modern technology habits. We are waiting for a phone call, waiting for the train, waiting for the walk sign. What do we do? Pull out the phone and desperately try to fill this time with something to bust the boredom. One widely circulated survey claimed that the average social media consumer spends 116 minutes per day on these sites. If correct, this is an amazing number given that this category of time did not exist twenty-five years ago. Where did the time come from? I have no idea. Time stretches to accommodate what people find interesting to do.

The bigger issue is that those minutes don't happen in a solid, mindful chunk. They dribble out through the day, turning what could be uninterrupted downtime into plugged-in time that feels sort of like work (people often check their email when they open their phones) but isn't. It's schedule clutter. It seems more productive than doing nothing, but is often worse.

Consciously choosing not to fill time with such boredom busters requires discipline, but it is probably the best thing you can do to feel like you have all the time in the world.

I saw this clearly in my time-diary study. I asked people to think back on their recent waking hours and estimate how frequently they checked their phones. The people in the top 20 percent of time-perception scores estimated on average 5.35 times per hour; people in the bottom 20 percent estimated 8.5. As for those in the bottom 3 percent? It was nearly 13 times per hour.

There could be a correlation issue here (and estimates are not the same thing as actually keeping track). The need to check email often initiates a phone check, and maybe people with less demanding jobs feel like they can check email less often. But other research has found causation. For a study published in *Computers in Human Behavior* in 2015, researchers had one group of people check email three times per day, while another group could check their email whenever. After a week, the groups switched instructions. The finding was that the same person, checking email less frequently, feels more relaxed than when he checks it more. This is true even though not checking email for a few hours raises the possibility of missing things, which in theory could be stressful.

I tend to think electronic connectivity in itself can lead to anxiety. I asked my survey respondents what they were most likely to do before bed on weekdays. People with the highest time-perception scores were about half as likely to surf the web or check social media as people with the lowest scores. They were far more likely to read or spend time with friends and family that they knew in real life, not via Instagram posts. Looking at their time as a whole, people in the top 20 percent reported about half as many minutes spent on social media or internet browsing as people in the bottom 20 percent. They felt less compulsion to fill space with electronic distractions. They knew that reading that listicle called "13 Ways to Turbo-Charge Your Productivity" would do less for their lives (or, frankly, their productivity) than sitting with their thoughts.

The reason modern types feel so busy, and yet have such trouble getting things done, is that we let ourselves become dependent on constant stimuli. We *like* being plugged in. It's easy entertainment, and we can avoid the need to entertain ourselves.

I was thinking of this at one of Sam's Little League games not long ago. It was a gorgeous spring day. Baseball progresses at a leisurely pace, particularly with little kids who have trouble hitting and catching, so there wasn't much going on. I was by myself (a treat!), so I wasn't chasing any of his siblings. I could have gone for a walk, or I could have reclined "cool-bedded in the flowery grass," as John Keats wrote in his "Ode on Indolence." I could have stared at the clouds, thinking deep thoughts, or no thoughts. Instead, I was doing what many other parents were doing: scrolling around on my phone, deleting newsletters someone subscribed me to, and reading repetitive political commentary that did not improve my mood.

Why? Forget sanctimonious clucking about paying attention to children's sports; my kid was having a conversation with a fellow outfielder about Pokémon, and he wasn't paying attention either. The truth is that I was bored. I didn't have the discipline to let myself move through boredom to the thoughts and reflections that arise when given fallow space. I had time, and I chose to fill it with the equivalent of gunk on the gears.

It seems harmless enough, but the problem is that then we are not aware that this space exists. It is chopped up for no good reason. No, I wasn't relaxing on a sunny Saturday afternoon. I was . . . working? Reading? Maintaining my personal brand? Or something. Then we believe the lie that we have no time.

Don't buy it. The truth is that even ten minutes spent looking at the sky with nothing to fill the time can feel long. Whether it feels pleasingly long or recklessly long depends on your attitude and what else is weighing on you. In Edith Wharton's words, the bustling Pauline Manford of *Twilight Sleep* fretted that "an hour is too long for meditation—an hour is too long for any-thing. Now that she had one to herself, for the first time in years, she didn't in the least know what to do with it. That was some-thing which no one had ever thought of teaching her."

But we can teach ourselves. Try it sometime. Baby steps are fine at first:

- Put the phone in airplane mode while you're with a friend.

- Leave it at home if you run to the corner store for some-thing.

- Put down this book and just breathe and look at some-thing beautiful.

If you try the last suggestion, aim to wait at least ten min-utes. Did it fly by? Probably not. When you picked up your phone to check the time, I'm guessing it showed that less than ten minutes had passed.

Open space feels heavy at first. But I'll wager nothing much changed in your world in that time. The earth kept spinning without your attention. Maybe the phone can stay in airplane mode longer. An hour. Two hours. A day. When I was leading a webinar recently, some people spoke admiringly of a colleague who managed to take a completely off-the-grid weeklong vaca-tion every summer. They marveled that he hadn't worried about emergencies. I noted that, vacations or not, we were all still there, four years later. Likely there were emergencies those summers. Four years on, no one has any clue what they were. But he had taken his break, and no doubt felt, during those weeks, that he had time and space for the things he wanted to do.

This is the spirit of that Mary Oliver poem "Summer Day." Everyone quotes the last line: "Tell me, what is it you plan to do with your one wild and precious life?" But that question comes after a meditation on a pleasant day spent doing little of life-altering consequence: kneeling in the grass with the insects, feeling idle and blessed. "Tell me, what else should I have done? Doesn't everything die at last, and too soon?"

Doing something is not always better than doing nothing. There is no point in deleting those emails. Let them be. Leave the phone. Don't fill time. Open it up—and though we may all die at last anyway, at least the time we have before then will feel as plentiful as summer light.

FOUR

LINGER

Where is it, this present? It has melted in our grasp, fled ere we could touch it, gone in the instant of becoming.

—William James, *The Principles of Psychology*

KJ Dell'Antonia, the author of *How to Be a Happier Parent* and a regular contributor to the *New York Times*, lives in rural New Hampshire. She and her husband have four children who play competitive ice hockey. This turns winter weeks into a blizzard of practices and games that require driving to rinks all over snowy New England.

Anything involving winter weather and unfamiliar turf is ripe for being late and rushing. For a long time, Dell'Antonia was late and rushing, but a few years ago she kicked that habit. This required learning to be realistic. "Late is you not taking into account the thing you know they're going to do," she says. It is a law of family dynamics that a child will plan to grab some element of hockey equipment, then remember that she needs to go to the bathroom, and do that, then walk straight out the door without the critical item, and remember it ten miles down the road. In her quest to stop being late, Dell'Antonia began figuring out what needed to be in the car long before they loaded up or, as her children grew older, making it clear that she expected them to have what they needed—there would be no turning around. The family left long before she might once have deemed necessary. She stopped trying to squeeze in one more activity (unloading the dishwasher?) before running out the door.

All was good. She loved being on time. She loved being *early* rather than being that family that was always racing in, apologizing for being unable to find the rink. Then in 2017, following a common practice in the blogging world, she decided to adopt a word for the year. Such a word is supposed to influence decisions and reinforce good habits. "I want to take my time," she says. She wanted a word that would sum up her new approach to life.

But what would that word be?

This was a surprisingly difficult linguistic puzzle. "Most words around taking time, spending time, going more slowly, have this negative connotation," she says. Blame whatever cultural forces you will, but she's not wrong. "Dillydally. Dawdle. They're all bad. They're all things you say to a recalcitrant toddler."

She tried on "mindful" for size, but that didn't quite match the concept she was going for. Nor was she trying to "enjoy each moment"—a frustrating goal if there ever was one. Says Dell'Antonia, "I have this image of a person patting you on the head in the supermarket saying, 'Enjoy every minute! It goes so fast!'" It is impossible to enjoy every minute, and taking care of four children just multiplies the odds of intermittent misery. "I want to enjoy the *enjoyable* moments," Dell'Antonia clarifies.

And so, finally, she settled on "linger." "Lingering is the opposite of rushing," she says. It feels more grown-up and luxurious than dawdling and dillydallying. It doesn't imply that you have nothing to do or that you are avoiding the important stuff. It implies that you have important things to do and you are giving them the time they deserve. And so she announced on her podcast and blog that 2017 would be the year of lingering.

Of course, having a theme and incorporating it into life are different matters. But Dell'Antonia found a few practical ways to linger in the hour-by-hour rhythm of deadlines and rinks.

First, if she finds herself enjoying something, she will stay with it. Her family eats dinner together most nights, but "together" means people coming in shifts as hockey practices end. "I've been making more of an effort to stay through the second shift, which I've found encourages other people to keep sitting there," she says. "We're just kind of sitting there, but it's nice." They talk about their days. They talk about hockey. Good conversation is better than rushing to get to the dishes. If she's enjoying an article, she'll read all the way to the end rather than thinking, *Hey, this is long. Shouldn't I be doing something else?*

Second, she's learned to view her weekend trips to hockey games as an opportunity for lingering as well. If they've bothered to drive somewhere, she notes, "Afterward, I look around. We're somewhere we're not usually." So what can they explore in these exotic locales? In Manchester, they found a chocolate shop that they now stop by anytime someone has a game there. As they lingered and asked questions, the proprietor informed them that he makes all his chocolates by hand and doesn't make any of the special flavors more than once because he gets bored. They hunt for good bookstores. Instead of trying to fit other things into the day, she thinks, *Let's just have this be the one thing we're doing and spend as much time as it takes.*

Finally, she's learned to make a mental switch. "The brain naturally focuses on the negative," she says. No one wants to get eaten by wild animals, so no doubt our ancestors did better when they loped around on something akin to high alert. But, as Dell'Antonia points out, the result is that "I'll just be driving along, with my teeth clenched and shoulders up." Why? If she isn't late, and no one is arguing, then she'll say, "Hold up: there is nothing wrong."

There is nothing wrong. Sometimes you really do have to call attention to this. All is OK. You can linger and enjoy what is actually an enjoyable moment. "Having the word really does help," she says. "Part of me is always thinking, *What am I supposed to do now? What is my next move? What am I supposed to do?* If the answer is 'lingering,' then that's a good answer."

Dwelling in the Present

I confess that I have a similar problem to Dell'Antonia's clenched teeth. As I began to study time perception, I noticed that I would often find myself wondering how long I had until the next thing. This was understandable in certain circumstances, such as if I needed to make it to a meeting on time, but I found myself doing this even when nothing was wrong and the transition to the next thing was obvious. On a flight to California, for instance, I found myself continually wondering when my five hours would be over. I am not sure why. I had no power to make the plane go faster. It would be obvious when we were landing. The driver who was meeting me at the airport would be watching the plane's arrival time, and I had nothing else I needed to do that evening anyway. I had no fidgety children to keep quiet. I was reading a good book. I wasn't hungry or tired or otherwise massively uncomfortable. While I might have preferred to be reading in an easy chair with more leg room, I had purchased a serviceable glass of wine from the American Airlines beverage cart. There was no real problem.

So why wasn't I happier?

The truth is that enjoying the present isn't easy. For starters, as William James notes, it is fleeting. It melts in our grasp. It flees as we try to touch it. Such mystery intrigues people, and the exact length of this fleeting present was, in James's day, a subject of excited experimental inquiry. Working memory might encompass a maximum period of about twelve seconds. The senses cannot distinguish between two events that are less than a certain fraction of a second apart. So it seems that the present is a duration somewhere in there, though this has an element that sounds, to modern ears, like inquiries into how many angels can dance on the head of a pin.

In any case, it is hard to revel in something that by the time you can identify it has already become a memory.

Another problem: we experience the present in our temporal bodies. This means that complete bliss is seldom possible.

This might strike a consumer of motivational quotes as a problem, given the number of Instagram posts with the Katy Perry lyric "All we have is this moment." In reality, enjoying the present need not come at the expense of thinking of the past or the future, a false choice that masquerades as deep thought in motivational literature. Indeed, thinking about the past and the future can enhance the experience of the present in profound ways.

That said, lingering does require a certain mind-set, and certain practices.

People who feel like time is abundant approach the present in two ways. First, the practical: they learn to be where they're supposed to be in enough time that they can relax. Then, the more daring psychological feat: they find ways to savor the space of time where they currently are, even if the present does flee, gone in that moment of becoming.

How to Never Be Late Again

First, in our inquiry into how we feel about the time right now, we turn to the practical topic of punctuality. For many people, the time right now is always twenty minutes behind what they had scheduled.

I have long been curious about this from an anthropological perspective, and occasionally an annoyed personal perspective, as I'm waiting for someone in a coffee shop.

I am generally punctual. Scratch that. I'm often comically early. So are many people who fall into the "upholder" category that author Gretchen Rubin outlines in her book about personality types, *The Four Tendencies*. Upholders are people who meet all outer and inner expectations, as opposed to questioners or rebels, who might have a more lackadaisical approach to what other people expect from them. (Obligers, the final tendency, meet outer expectations but not inner ones. These are the people who could show up daily for track practice in high school but can't make themselves run as adults.)

We upholders know that other people are waiting for us, or at least theoretically might be waiting for us (even if we know the other party routinely texts "on way" when he just got out of the shower). Failing to meet this expectation feels so painful that we view an appointed time as a line in the sand we may not cross. Hence my tendency to show up awkwardly early for parties. Rubin has written that this "upholder" category includes her too. I'd wager it includes anyone who writes books on productivity, which always makes get-togethers of such writers a humorous exercise. A 10:00 A.M. meeting may as well start at 9:50. Once, when Rubin and I were both in Austin, she and I planned to interview each other via Facebook Live. Twelve minutes before we were supposed to meet in her hotel lobby, she texted me, "I'm on my way! May be a few mins late!" I was somewhat surprised, but I continued on to our meeting spot and, being about seven minutes early as I always am, I settled in to answer emails while I waited. The punch line: a text followed two minutes later saying, "Upholder panic! I'm on time." She walked into the lobby about thirty seconds after that. We were both there well before the time we'd arranged to meet.

As someone who's often early, I assumed for a long time that people who were chronically late were rude. They valued their own time over mine. They made me wait so they didn't have to.

I do still think this is the case with some people, and some understaffed service firms and medical offices. Some other head-in-the-clouds types manage to walk around with smartphones and smart watches and clocks on their microwaves, coffeemakers, dashboards, and even highway billboards and still be *completely unaware of the time.*

As I've studied people's schedules, though, I've seen that there's often something else going on. Many chronically late people are people pleasers. If someone takes more time than he asked for, the chronically tardy don't feel comfortable ending what's going on to move to something else. That's lingering in a way, though it's often an overcommitted lingering.

Late people tend to be wildly optimistic. They think it takes thirty minutes to get to work because it did once at 5:00 A.M., but the trip normally happens at 8:00 A.M., when traffic is worse. This wild optimism also keeps people from building all the constituent parts of an activity into their mental picture. Even if they know roughly how long it will take to go buy groceries, they don't factor in unloading the car and putting the groceries away, even though they do these activities every time they buy groceries. This incomplete picture means they're constantly behind.

Being optimistic isn't a bad way to go through life. Focusing on the person in front of you regardless of time can be a good thing if the person truly needs it (though it can be a bad thing if other people abuse it). Regardless, these tendencies do make people late. And while some antisocial sorts view their being late as a power play, normal nonpsychopathic late people hate being late. They hate apologizing to the same people for the fourteenth time. Knowing you are disappointing and angering someone feels bad enough that people will forget their broader obligations to humanity to avoid the feeling. Late people speed through residential neighborhoods. They cause crashes by running red lights. In one famous experiment, seminary students asked to deliver a talk on the Good Samaritan—who is in the Bible because he stopped to help an injured man—were highly likely *not* to stop to help an injured person when told that they were late to deliver their talks. While I appreciate the researchers' sense of humor, this doesn't speak well of human nature.

People who feel rushed and harried are, by definition, more likely to feel like time is moving too fast. The best way to avoid this frantic feeling is to *stop being late*. I do believe that the majority of the time this is within people's control, and that most of the things that make people late—traffic, lost shoes, a colleague who just grabbed you to chat—are entirely predictable. They are *known unknowns*. Yes, I know lateness is somewhat in the eye of the beholder. If you're invited to a dinner party in much of Latin America, showing up at the stated time is rude to your hosts. But if you feel "late" all the time it is because you recognize there is a gap between expectations and performance, whatever the expectations happen to be, and the fact that you recognize the expectations means the situation isn't hopeless.

There are many reasons to track time. Seeing how long things take is one. If, in your mind, it takes fifteen minutes to get to church and it takes twenty-five minutes most times you go, then this explains why you're ten minutes late for every service except that one (which you keep remembering!). In your mind your workday might end at 5:30 P.M., but if your time log shows that you rarely leave the office before 6:00 P.M., this explains why you're generally late for your Tuesday-night volunteering gig that starts at 6:30 P.M.

If you don't want to track your time, or you're dealing with some unknown activity, then just add in extra time. When I study the schedules of punctual people, this is almost always what they're doing, even if the process has become so automatic they barely think about it.

Andrew Glincher, CEO and managing partner of law firm

Nixon Peabody, and a fellow punctual soul, has never missed a flight. He is never late for meetings, a fact I can attest to after interviewing him a few times. "I think it's a respect issue," he says. And so, "I prepare to arrive fifteen minutes before." He and his assistant strategize to avoid running behind; if he suspects his 3:00 P.M. meeting will definitely run the full hour, he won't set the next meeting until 4:30 P.M. He learned the habit from his father, a taxi driver who dealt with enough traffic nonsense during working hours that he didn't want to be flummoxed by it on the weekend too. When the elder Glincher took young Andrew to baseball games, they'd arrive at the ballpark at 11:00 A.M. for a 2:00 P.M. start. The upside was "we didn't have to pay for parking!" These days, Glincher makes sure to leave his desk several minutes before he actually needs to leave his desk to get to the train on time. The reason? He knows people will stop him in the halls to talk. The extra time means he can have real conversations instead of racing off.

A fifteen-minute buffer is good for most everyday activities, but if you're dealing with a bigger chunk of time, the buffer should get proportionally bigger too. KJ Dell'Antonia used to see that a hockey rink was one hour and fifteen minutes away, so she'd think to leave the house one hour and fifteen minutes before they needed to be there. But getting in the car takes some nonzero amount of time, and then they'd already be late. If anything went wrong en route, they'd be quite late, and then they'd be hunting for the right place to park, and the right locker room, and the whole experience would be more unpleasant than it needed to be. She eventually learned that it was better to aim to leave two hours before. She'd get out the door at T minus 1:50, and then if she needed to stop for gas or if someone got hungry, she could swing by a grocery store to grab something healthy and filling rather than gas station Skittles. If she got there early, she could take her time to find the right spot, and then do something with the found time, such as call a friend or read a book. While it might feel wasteful (I could have emptied the dishwasher!), chronically late people can be so far off in their estimates that what they think will make them early means they're on time.

Of course, even with realistic estimates, lateness happens. Mental models can encompass things in the 10 to 90 percent probabilities, but not highly unlikely events. Traffic on the way to work is expected. You do not expect that a truck carrying printer ink will turn over and spill its contents, and that the resulting slick will shut down the Pennsylvania Turnpike. The good news is that if you're generally on time, people will understand the few times that you aren't. They know something out of the ordinary happened because your lateness is out of the ordinary.

If you are late, regardless of the cause, and you are disappointing someone, expressing contrition is the right thing to do. What is not right to do: putting yourself and everyone else in danger in an attempt to save ninety seconds. Pull over, call, apologize, and continue on your way. Rather than being fifteen minutes late and a hot mess, you're twenty minutes late but calm enough to solve the problem your tardiness caused.

Learn to Savor

That's how to stop being late. But lingering isn't just about ending the rushing caused by knowing you are supposed to be somewhere ten miles away and you aren't even in your car. It is about actively savoring the present, and thus stretching your experience of time.

To savor is to feel pleasure, and also to appreciate that you are feeling pleasure. It takes normal gratification and adds a second layer to it, acknowledgment. That this appreciation expands time can be understood by thinking of the opposite. When you want time to pass quickly, you might wish yourself elsewhere. When you want to prolong something, you hold yourself right where you are. Survey respondents who strongly agreed that they felt present rather than distracted the day before were 35 percent more likely than average to say that they generally had time for things that they wanted to do.

Being present means thinking about what is going on. It means taking in your surroundings. You know it still cannot last forever, as nothing lasts forever. You become like Mrs. Ramsay in *To the Lighthouse*, taking in the end of her triumphant dinner party. "With her foot on the threshold she waited a moment longer in a scene which was vanishing even as she looked," Virginia Woolf wrote. You know you are watching the present enter the past. Yet still you stand there watching the fading. You savor the moment. You *linger*.

This concept of savoring—a word much like lingering, with a slightly more pleasurable connotation—turns out to be a critical component in the field of positive psychology. Psychologists have long studied how resilient people learn to cope with difficulty. But it is an equally interesting adaptation to learn how to savor the good. Some people can take a good experience and take steps to make it richer and last longer.

Intriguingly, the richest experiences of savoring involve an awareness of the past and the future, as well as the present. In their 2006 book *Savoring: A New Model of Positive Experience,* two of the leading researchers in this field, Fred B. Bryant and the late Joseph Veroff, share Bryant's account of summiting 14,000-plus-foot Snowmass Mountain in the Colorado Rockies. He was in awe of the physical grandeur, of course, the snow-capped peaks looking like a frozen sea where "wave after wave of silver-tipped crests merge with green-blanketed valleys in the distant haze." He and his friends stood silent, marveling. But Bryant also knew he would likely never be there again. He had already tried to summit Snowmass twice and failed, and so he did more than just enjoy the view. He embraced his friends and told them how happy he was to share this moment with them. He looked back into the past, recalling a back injury that had almost ended his climbing career. He let his mind go to a time when he thought he would never experience this moment. "The realization that it is here now intensifies my joy," he thought. He projected himself forward into the future, and thought about how he might look back on this memory. He thanked God for enabling him to be there, and for creating mountains to climb.

Then with "a strong sense of the fleetingness of the moment" and a desire "to remember this moment" for the rest of his life, he made special efforts to capture the scene. He turned in a deliberate circle and recorded small details: a forest of aspen and spruce, a river down below. He noticed how his lungs felt, what he was smelling. He felt the cold. He selected a stone from the summit to bring down as a souvenir. He thought of sharing the memory of the mountain with his loved ones, and even thought of his late grandfather, who also loved outdoor adventures. He thought of how proud he would be of him. Bryant and his companions weren't on the summit long—the weather shifted and they had to get down—but all this savoring made the experience seem more vast than the ten minutes he later told me it encompassed.

Down off the mountain—and thinking about psychology in general—Bryant worked with his co-researcher Veroff to learn more about how people savor happy moments. Scanning the past and imagining the future were intimately part of the experience: "A conceptual model of savoring must consider not only reminiscence, but also anticipatory processes," they wrote. They produced the "Ways of Savoring Checklist," which they used to evaluate how different people hold on to experiences. For what is essentially a research document in an academic book, it's a surprisingly practical tool kit of dozens of strategies people can use to hold on to the moment. For instance:

- You can think about sharing the memory later with other people, or consciously taking in every scent during the event.

- You might remind yourself how long you had waited for this event to happen, or think back to a time when the event hadn't happened and you really wanted it to.

- You might try to become more alert, take deep breaths, or slow down.

- You might tell anyone else there how much you value the moment and how happy you are that the other people are there with you.

- You could remind yourself that nothing lasts forever. And so, you must enjoy this moment now.

Any good event can be deepened in these simple, doable ways. Yet the brain is often at odds with itself. Along with strategies for savoring, Bryant and Veroff identified what they called "Kill-Joy Thinking" tactics. These are ways people undermine their enjoyment of the moment. As with tardiness, there is a cultural component here. Confucianism, for instance, values avoiding extremes, and as an extension of that, cultures influenced by Confucianism may teach that too much heady enjoyment prompts the universe to even itself out. People deliberately minimize certain moments of happiness to set all right with the world. Other people may have a brain chemistry excuse; the cognitive distortion that is a hallmark of depression leads people experiencing this chemical imbalance to take any good thing and run it into the ground. It could have been better; it could have lasted longer; it could have happened earlier; I didn't deserve it.

But plenty of people who don't have these excuses engage in ways of ending the buzz. One of the most potent ways people keep themselves from lingering and savoring? Thinking about other places they should be or other things they should be doing. As Bryant said when I interviewed him in 2017, "Generally, our minds are elsewhere."

I think this almost comically common tendency of the human mind gets at the real wisdom in the "all we have is this moment" posts on social media. If you're on the mountain, you aren't going to be able to pay your electric bill until you descend enough to reach a spot with wi-fi. So why think about it? People tell me that they have no time to relax. I look at their time logs and see an entry such as "massage" on a Saturday morning. The person will rue that yes, that happened, but she was thinking about her in-box the whole time.

Cultivating the Savoring Habit

Savoring is not easy. Nor is it always possible. If you've got to be on the 7:34 A.M. train for work, you can't linger over that cup of coffee you brewed at 7:15 A.M. But lingering isn't all or nothing. Even if some moments don't lend themselves to lingering, others do, and this mental discipline can have a profound effect on the perception of time. As Bryant and Veroff put it, "Savoring seems to go hand in hand with the experience of time passing more slowly."

There are many ways to cultivate this habit. While humans have the ability to undermine their happiness even on a mountaintop, the advantage of such a place is that you know it is supposed to be incredible. That's why people climb mountains. That's why they pay attention while they're up there. Bryant reports that he still keeps the stone he grabbed from the Snowmass summit on his desk. "I can sniff it at any time. It smells like the top," he says. "I can close my eyes and go right back there."

It is harder to notice the ordinary good in ordinary moments. Bryant, who calls savoring "an acquired skill," has his tactics. He teaches psychology classes at Loyola University Chicago. In my experience, professors sometimes grumble about teaching undergraduates. Bryant, on the other hand, envisions himself at a nursing home someday in the future. In this vision, his health is failing. He can no longer get around on his own. He pictures himself in this state looking back on his life and wishing he could be in front of a classroom again, feeling healthy and mentally alert. All those sharp young minds are eager to hear from him. *Oh, what he would give for just one more day.* Then he opens his eyes and realizes, "That's today!" He doesn't have to give up anything to get this privilege! He gets to teach! This constructed contrast—something akin to George Bailey getting his second chance in *It's a Wonderful Life*—awakens him to the joys of normalcy. "There are so many ways to use the mind as a time machine," he says. "Mental time travel is so beautiful and rich."

Dell'Antonia began pointing out to herself that "there is nothing wrong." When I have moments like on the plane, I pause and note that "I am not unhappy now." The negative framing in both our mantras is key. If a negative state is assumed in life, then you have to call attention to its absence. "Bad stuff will kick your door in and force you to deal with it," says Bryant. "But the good stuff doesn't kick your door in and come after you. You have to find it and wrestle with it. It's a much more subtle set of skills." Even around the dinner table, if the kids are not screaming or if Alex is happily watching *Go, Diego, Go!* and I am able to read for a few minutes on the Kindle app, I can notice that I am enjoying the present moment. This acknowledgment that something is pleasant, and you are experiencing that pleasure, is the definition of savoring. And because noticing is part of the definition of savoring, it follows that a savored moment doesn't pass unnoticed. It does not slip into what William James called the "bottomless abyss of oblivion."

You can also engineer lingering moments. One reason to clear the calendar of what you don't want to do is so you can linger if you're having a good time with the things you do want to do. An after-work happy hour can turn into dinner. A planned ten-mile bike ride on an out-and-back trail can become sixteen miles if the weather is nice. I love to create completely open days when all I do is write. There is no watching the clock to make sure I don't miss a phone call. I will reconstruct my day at the end for my time log (well, probably in the middle when my body forces me to take breaks), but in the meantime, I'm off the clock and savoring a project I'm really getting into.

If setting aside a whole day is not possible, and I recognize that few people can engineer a day with no interruptions, you can still try what Bryant and Veroff named the "Daily Vacation Exercise" to practice lingering in pleasurable experiences. Each day, for one week, plan to do something you find enjoyable for ten to twenty minutes. A few possibilities are:

- watching the sunset,

- sitting outside at a café with a good cup of coffee,

- visiting a bookstore on your lunch break, or

- going for a walk in a nearby park.

Bryant reports that some recent daily vacations for him have included playing the guitar, composing music, walking his dog, and calling an old friend. "Or I might plan my next mountain climbing trip."

Choose a time when you can minimize distractions. You've put the phone in airplane mode or holstered it in its charger. During your daily vacation, per Bryant and Veroff, "try to notice and explicitly acknowledge to yourself each stimulus or sensation that you find pleasurable. Identify your positive feelings and explicitly label them in your mind. Actively build a memory of the feeling and the stimuli associated with it, close your eyes, swish the feeling around in your mind, and outwardly express the positive feeling in some way." Then plan tomorrow's daily vacation. At the end of the week, recall all seven vacations.

The truth is that we take at least ten-minute breaks in normal life anyway. We just fill this time by deleting emails. Or we scroll through social media, or putter around our houses. Then this doesn't register as leisure time. Consciously lingering in pleasurable downtime reminds us that we have downtime. And that can make us feel like we have more time than when we let it slip through our hands.

Finally, if you don't have to move fast, try moving slow. Not all activities require speed. If rushing makes people feel like they lack time for things they want to do, then conscious deliberation can feel like a treat. Bryant reports that in the lab, when subjects are given a chocolate-chip cookie and told to max out on their enjoyment of it, they almost universally slow down from a normal eating pace. They try to notice each bite fully. The reason is obvious: "Slowing down makes it last longer. The enjoyment itself is sustained."

Moving slowly also allows you to pay attention to more

things. "Slowing down is a conscious effort, so you're controlling the experience, and you're becoming more aware of what's going on," says Bryant. Part of the joy of mountain climbing is that you move so slowly in the thin air that you have time to take in all the details. You notice patterns in the moss on rocks, the hum of insects. Bryant reports that on a recent climbing trip he found himself admiring near-microscopic alpine flowers with petals smaller than a match head. "We marvel at that, but it's only because we stopped to look. You don't notice things like that if you're speeding through."

This slowness can be as delicious as a savored cookie. I might read more slowly through a book if I am enjoying it. There is pleasure in figuring out how something ends, but there is also pleasure in rereading a few sentences of choice prose.

Again, I wish to stress that not all parts of life lend themselves to slowing down. Sometimes slowness is lingering, and sometimes it is just dillydallying. My default speed is fast, and I make no apologies for this. Being OK with quick transitions when that's required makes my life possible.

Furthermore, not all situations deserve lingering. Frequent flyers learn to arrive at the gate just in time to board. Small children and their short attention spans naturally reduce the time spent on many activities. By myself I might spend hours in an art museum. Taking a kid I will aim for an hour and feel lucky if we make that. As I've read about the Scandinavian concepts of *hygge* (Denmark) and *koselig* (Norway), which have to do with relaxation and lingering, I am reminded that many ideas for living the good life are harder to implement if you have toddlers. In 2017's *The Little Book of Hygge,* Meik Wiking waxes eloquently about lingering over a board game on a wintry weekend day for fourteen hours. I have no doubt this is a lovely way to spend time with good friends, good food, and good drinks. A fire roaring in the fireplace helps. I also know that many people reading this book could pull off a fourteen-hour board game only if they dropped the kids at Grandma's for the weekend. It is hard to linger in the moment if you're trying to keep a small child from leaping into the fireplace.

Consequently, much of the literature telling people to slow down and smell the roses may as well be like the old man in the grocery store telling you to enjoy every moment. It is impossible. Worse, it adds insult to injury by making you feel like you are a bad person for noticing that life has tough moments.

Instead, lingering is about enjoying the enjoyable. It is about understanding that you have the power to stretch time when you are in it and when you wish to stretch it. All time passes, and you cannot linger in anything forever. Hedonic adaptation—the human tendency to become accustomed to anything—means that even a view from the mountaintop becomes the scene out the kitchen window after a while. But for a few minutes, with the right mind-set, it can be more.

I was thinking of this one night after reading Alex his bedtime stories. I sat rocking him in his dark room for quite a while. Through his young life, he has rarely fallen asleep easily. (More on that in the next chapter.) I knew as soon as I left that he would leave his bed, and go howl at the door for me until he fell asleep on the floor. Even on his most tired nights, he needed to get in his howling, just to register his disapproval of the whole bedtime affair. Then he would exhaust himself enough to sleep, and I would come move him back to his bed.

It was never pleasant. A philosopher might have much to say about what this nightly ritual my son enacted means for the human condition. But even knowing what was coming, I could expand the space before that screaming. I could linger with his little pajama-clad body pressed against mine, pondering that I probably do not have many more nights like this. Some lonely day in the future I might wish that I could have a child snuggled up against me, and that my arms might be strong enough to hold him. Lingering can be bittersweet. This fourth baby has been a bit of a terror. But in the nursery, for a moment, there was nothing but peace.

FIVE

INVEST IN YOUR HAPPINESS

Happiness in intelligent people is the rarest thing I know.
—Ernest Hemingway, *The Garden of Eden*

A scene plays out at a Waffle House in suburban Atlanta several mornings a week. Visit in the early hours, and you'll spot Chris Carneal in his usual booth toward the back. Despite the name of the establishment, there will probably not be waffles at his table, only eggs and bacon, but there will be papers, or his laptop, or a book, or sometimes a companion.

The time is a little after 6:00 A.M. This is already stage two in Carneal's morning routine. He wakes at 4:55 A.M. He is in the car at 5:02 A.M. to zip over to a 5:15 A.M. class at a CrossFit gym near his house. He spends the next forty-five minutes pounding out his workout of the day. Then he heads to the nearby Waffle House, where the staff doesn't mind Carneal's workout gear, his lingering, or, seemingly, that he doesn't order waffles.

It is nothing fancy, but it solves what could be a big problem in a busy man's life.

Carneal is the founder and CEO of Boosterthon, a company that assists schools with fund-raising. Boosterthon has about four hundred full-time and two hundred part-time employees. Most are on the young side; for many it is their first "real" job. Even many managers are new to the working world, and need an accessible boss. Carneal and his wife also have four young children, with all the school functions and activities that number implies. With so many people who want his attention, he could easily feel frazzled and pulled in many directions.

Instead, his early-morning workouts, and then the Waffle House, present a different option—one in which by investing time in activities he truly wants to do first and, conveniently, by doing them while the rest of his family is asleep, he can feel less busy yet still get more done.

He shows up at the Waffle House at 6:05 A.M. He spends five to seven minutes praying and reflecting. He looks at the day's schedule. Then, he says, "I try to dedicate the rest of that hour to the one big thing I'm thinking about. How do I drive the business forward? What's the next big idea or market we could take, and what are my questions about it?" Once a week someone might join him for a more cerebral chat than could happen during the day. He wraps up at 7:20 A.M. and heads home to spend the next forty-five minutes with the kids before school. Then he'll work another hour and change at the house (grabbing a quick shower in there too).

The result: by the time he shows up at the office around 9:30 or 10:00 A.M., he's put in 2.5 hours of solid, focused work. "My mind is alive, and I'm ready to go," he says. "In those 2.5 hours, I get more done than I used to in a six-, seven-, eight-hour day."

Then there's this change: In the past, before instituting his morning ritual, he would often feel distracted at work. He would have trouble fully engaging in conversations with team members who came to see him because he would be thinking of the other problems he still needed to address. He would be wondering when the conversations would end, so that he could get back to those problems, hoping he would be able to deal with those problems before his family expected him home around 5:30 P.M. Now he doesn't show up at work until he's solved them. Having been proactive in the morning, he is "free to be reactive" at the office. "It gives me clarity through the day," he says. "I can walk slowly through the halls. I can high-five more people. I can feel fine when I'm interrupted." Because the truth is, when you're in management, those interruptions are your job. Or as Carneal puts it, "My team is my work."

This investment of time at the gym, the Waffle House, and home has made him happier and more relaxed. He can deal with the day as the day comes. Plus, putting the good stuff first seems to stretch time. "I look at my watch sometimes and think it's got to be 2:00 P.M.," says Carneal. "Then I find out, wow, it's only 10:30!"

The Link Between Happiness and Time

As we learned in chapter 2, when people say they want more time, what they often mean is that they want more *memories*. This chapter is about a second aspect of this. When people say they want more time, they also mean that they want *more time spent doing things they are happy about*. Few people would want more time tacked on to a prison sentence. Someone counting minutes as he's stuck in a traffic jam might say he wants more time, but he wants more time outside his car, not inside it. Otherwise, why count the minutes? Time is just time, but we perceive it differently based on what we are doing, and our mental state.

The good news is that the proportion of time spent on things that are satisfying versus things that are less so may be changeable over time. People who feel like they have enough time for the things they want to do make strategic choices to optimize their time. As we saw in chapter 3, this can mean creating time dividends: doing things now to open up space in the future. This chapter is likewise about paying in, with the goal of moving more moments into the "enjoyable" category. Often, this involves investing resources—money, for sure, but time is also a resource, and so is the mental energy required to develop a new worldview—in achieving happiness.

These three resources play their parts in different ways. Money is straightforward. Time is less so, though it can be a game changer: it is how Carneal gets more done around breakfast time than he used to in a day. Mind-set is the least understood resource of all of these, though it is probably the most profound. Being able to switch from enduring to enjoying, from counting minutes to seeing them as tolerable, has huge implications for opening up time. In the time-perception survey, people who strongly agreed with the statement "Yesterday, I spent my time in ways that made me happy" were 22 percent more likely to agree that they generally had time for the things that they wanted to do in life. People in the top 20 percent of time-perception scores spent a higher proportion of their time on things that are known mood boosters—exercise, reflective activities, and interacting with friends and family—as opposed to people in the bottom 20 percent of time-perception scores, who spent more time online and watching TV. These are activities whose pleasures turn out not to do much for people in the long run.

In any case, people with all the time in the world know that happiness is a worthy goal. Because how we live our hours is how we live our lives, being happy with our lives means being happy with our hours. Whether those hours are spent in a Waffle House or elsewhere, strategic investments can help us consciously design our lives to make us relaxed about our time or, if not happy, at least less unhappy than we would be.

How Money Can Buy Happiness

While we all have the same 168 hours in a week, people do not have the same amount of money, and when people hear "invest," that's the topic that comes to mind first. Consequently, the usual narratives of money and privilege bubble up, though intriguingly these narratives are often at odds. Can money buy happiness, or does the evidence come down on the "more money, more problems" side of the ledger? Is it only helpful to a point of diminishing returns?

What I think it's safest to say is that money is a tool. It will not automatically produce happiness, just as a hammer lying in a toolbox does nothing. Used strategically, it can enable a great deal.

Where people go awry on the money and happiness question is that we misjudge the nature of happiness. To quote Tolstoy, "Pure and complete sorrow is as impossible as pure and complete joy." Few good or bad bumps last long; we drift back to where we were. As Ruth observed to me in the CVS parking lot after I'd succumbed to her pleas to buy a doll from the clearance rack, "When you get a new toy, you're excited about it, but after a while, you don't play with it anymore." Purchases are most likely to make people happy if they enable enjoyable experiences, which can then become memories. These memories become ongoing fonts of pleasure, and are not subject to the same hedonic adaptation that plagues most seemingly pleasurable things in life. A tent buys happiness if you use it to go camping, and then during your commute you recall those crisp nights and crimson leaves. If it sits in your basement because you never make the time to use it, it won't.

Happiness can also be measured in many ways. There's life satisfaction, which is how you think life is going overall. There's nothing wrong with this measure, but one's mood is more often determined by that spoiled child known as the experiencing self. People can become upset at this disconnect. You find yourself thinking, *Of course I should be happy! I have a good job, a beautiful house.* But if you wake too early to endure a miserable commute between that beautiful house and your good job, and then you come home to spend the evening scrolling through Instagram photos of other people's slightly bigger and more beautiful houses, you will not feel blissful.

If we accept that moment-by-moment happiness is often driving our moods, then investing money strategically in producing happiness means understanding which activities induce happiness and which do not.

Studies of human happiness find that people are more likely to be in better moods during certain activities than during others. Sex, unsurprisingly, rates better than commuting to work. Indeed, the commute to work is, statistically, the low point of the average person's day. Commuting home from work scores better, presumably because one arrives home at the end of it, a redeeming factor absent from the morning run. Other activities might depend on the person. Work in general does not score well, but this is often the hour-by-hour problem again. You can love your colleagues and believe deeply in your organization's mission, and still find that Tuesday-morning staff meeting insufferable. Most people enjoy socializing and relaxing. Running errands in general scores low, but it depends on the errand. Some people really like grocery shopping, though many people dislike battling other shoppers in a crowded mega-store while trying to find a certain lightbulb that the store turns out not to carry. Childcare is likewise a mixed bag. Playing with kids can be fun. Refereeing sibling battles, not so much.

Investing money to achieve happiness requires analyzing pain points in how you spend your time, and figuring out what can be done about them. No one can truly make more time; once a second is gone, all the money in the world cannot lure it back. Yet money can change the proportion of aggravation to contentment in a life. When you can reduce time spent on things you don't enjoy doing—activities that have you counting the minutes, hoping they will be over soon—and increase the time spent on things you do enjoy doing, then you will feel like you have more time. When money can achieve this, then it is often money well spent.

If you decided to track your time after reading chapter 1, look at your log in this light. Ask yourself a few questions:

- When was I happy?

- When was I not happy?

- Could money change any of this?

- If so, how much would be required?

Sometimes this can involve major money decisions. If commuting is the low point of people's days, then spending money to reduce the time devoted to it could be a wise investment. Someone who rents a place close to work can spend his mornings lingering over breakfast, or putting in some time at the gym, rather than sitting in a parking lot on the interstate. If he moves close enough, he might be able to bike to work, thus turning what might be the low point of the day into something reasonably enjoyable.

As for work hours themselves, if these feel long sometimes, then officially trimming them could be a way to invest money in achieving happiness. Plenty of people would like to work part-time, including people who love their jobs. If your finances allow it, that can certainly open up space for other pursuits. The *Best of Both Worlds* podcast owes its existence to my cohost, Sarah Hart-Unger, electing to go to an 80 percent schedule in her primary job as a physician. On her day off, we record episodes, and she gets in a little more reading, exercising, and blogging time.

Of course, not all organizations or jobs are amenable to part-time work, and sometimes going off a full-time track can have far-reaching implications for a person's career. I find that part-time options tend to work best in careers (such as medicine) where hours are more set and you are either in the office or not. The danger in other kinds of salaried work, as my time-diary studies have found, is that if no one knows how many hours anyone is working, "part-time" can often mean full-time hours for less pay. If that sounds like the reality of your industry, it might be a more satisfying option to hunt for (or craft) a job you love, and then negotiate for flexible hours in lieu of extra cash. If you do elect to take a pay cut to go part-time, work out a schedule where you get real days off—for example, you don't go into the office Thursday or Friday—rather than accept vague promises of a reduced workload. This has the virtue of reducing work hours *and* commuting time too.

Outsourcing chores and errands you find stressful can be a good use of funds. Amazon Prime's two-day shipping eliminates the need to get in the car to buy random items such as coffee filters. Likewise, if you're gone from home a lot during the week, it doesn't make sense to spend your weekends mowing the lawn when many services will take care of this job. Spend the time relaxing, socializing, or going on day-trip adventures, and you'll feel like you have more time.

In my life, learning to use childcare strategically has been a big breakthrough for investing in my happiness. Sure, being able to focus while I'm working is great, as is enjoying the occasional dinner out with my husband at restaurants that don't have crayons. But what's been most transformative is realizing that childcare can let me do fun things *with* my kids that would be hard to do as a stay-at-home mother of a big brood. I can chaperone Ruth's field trips, even though they happen during Alex's nap time. I can guide Jasper through a school project while someone else drives Sam home from coding club. On a Saturday morning when one kid has a swim meet and another has a friend's birthday party, it is lovely to send one parent to each event and let the younger children stay home with someone who will build Lego towers with them. They're not miserable on the sidelines;

we're not miserable chasing them. This is an investment in life satisfaction.

Getting rid of pain points can do a lot to change the perception of time. But just as savoring means not just the absence of bad things but also stretching the good, investing in happiness means being willing to spend on joy.

On Treating Yourself

In the quest to enjoy more of my hours, I keep coming back to the concept of treats. Treats are little things that make a big difference in mood. These can involve small outlays of cash—such as buying that book you're dying to read instead of waiting for the library to get it—or even nonobvious ones, like a relaxing bath (you pay your water bill, but the connection isn't immediate).

We all have these things that perk us up, and yet if you are the sort of disciplined, frugal person who reads self-help books, I imagine you don't employ these tools as often as you could. That makes sense for unhealthy or expensive indulgences. But for most treats, this fear of hedonism is misplaced. Exactly what is gained by using the free pen from the bank when substituting a higher-end model might make writing your to-do list a pleasure?

Investing in your happiness means making more liberal use of these grown-up goodies. That's what I discovered one November when, needing to write some Thanksgiving-themed articles,

I decided to spend thirty days writing down three things daily I was grateful for. Sure, I became marginally more likely to look on the bright side of life. But the real breakthrough came on a lousy day when nothing was going right. I was gloomy as the gray sky, yet I realized around noon that I would have to write down three things that evening I was grateful for. That left me the rest of the day to engineer three wonderful things into my hours. I promptly left my computer, got in my car, and went for a trail run somewhere beautiful. It felt like playing hooky in the middle of the day for the price of a gallon of gas. Then I stopped at a favorite restaurant for takeout. I got a fun book and holed myself up with a glass of wine to read after the kids went to bed. Voilà: a good day, with hours spent doing happy things, winning the lottery not required.

Pay Yourself First

So that's money. But investing in happiness isn't just about cash. Time is also a resource. It too can be invested in ways that bring happiness and a sense of time freedom. What Chris Carneal saw is that while an hour is always an hour, the confluence of energy levels and other people's demands means that not all hours are equally suited to all things. If you wait until the end of the day to see what time is left over for the important stuff, the odds are good you won't have the energy to do anything but col-lapse into bed. If you're managing people—employees or little ones—even waiting until the middle of the day can result in you feeling pulled in many directions. Feeling harried and rushed is associated with feeling like you lack the time for the things you want to do. Doing what matters first opens up time.

That's the beauty of mornings. Anytime someone has grand ambitions but a lot on their plates, I suggest looking at morning hours for opportunities.

Choosing three mornings a week to wake up half an hour earlier and run for twenty-five minutes on a basement treadmill can open up hours of energy and focus for the price of this ninety minutes invested. (For what it's worth, people in the top 20 percent of time-perception scores exercised 3.4 times per week, compared with 1.9 times for those in the bottom 20 percent.)

If you want to write a novel, getting up an hour early four mornings a week and writing five hundred words on each of those mornings would give you a full-length draft in less than a year.

You can also use mornings for reflective and spiritual activities such as journaling, meditating, and praying. All of these are associated with feeling like time is abundant. In my survey, people in the top 20 percent of time-perception scores engaged in such activities 3.3 times per week, versus 1.4 times for those in the bottom 20 percent. Some 22 percent of the top tier engaged in these activities daily, versus 11 percent of survey takers overall. Nearly half of people in the bottom 20 percent reported *never* engaging in such activities.

Given that anyone can find five minutes a day to write in a journal, I'm inclined to believe that the reason for this link is not the obvious one: that people don't have time for these activities, so they don't do them. Instead, when people don't pause to reflect on their lives, they just move from thing to thing and don't notice how much time they have. Taking a few minutes each morning to step back and reflect can make the rest of the day feel spacious. This is a major win for such a small chunk of time change.

That's not to say that getting up earlier than you have to is easy. Sometimes investing in happiness requires a few moments of unhappiness. Carneal doesn't like waking up at 4:55 A.M., nor do all family situations, life stages, or chronotypes lend themselves to morning routines. Night owls may truly do their best work after sunset. But many people don't spend the hour before bed all that well. If you're just puttering around the house or looking at photos on social media of people you're not that fond of, you might try cutting off the puttering earlier, going to bed earlier, and turning unproductive evening hours into productive morning hours.

If something important has to happen, it has to happen first. This same philosophy can be applied to the week as well.

My accountability partner, Katherine Reynolds Lewis, has long had an impressive journalism career. She was meeting her income goals writing about parenting, business, and other things, but when we started checking in on each other in early 2013, she told me that what she really wanted to do was write a book. She decided to allocate Friday afternoons to researching and writing pitches for meatier magazine stories that could turn into book proposal fodder. Because Friday afternoon is a low opportunity cost time—most editors and sources weren't calling her then—it seemed like the perfect spot for speculative matters.

But it wasn't. Week after week, she would confess to me that she'd spent little time on this career-advancing work. As she explains, "The problem with Friday afternoons was that all the incomplete tasks of the week—both professional and personal—piled up into that last two hours of Friday. So by the time my desk was clear, it was 4:00 P.M. or 5:00 P.M. and it felt futile to tackle something new."

As we discussed the situation, we decided that she should move her pitch writing to first thing Monday morning. Monday morning is the start of the week. It is often people's best time, and it's time that's unlikely to be lost to emergencies, because the emergencies have yet to stack up.

As we talked about this, I knew it was going to be a radical, even uncomfortable idea. Lewis was going to be purposefully postponing assigned work with deadlines and dollars attached to do unpaid work that might never pan out. Obviously she hoped it would lead to something, but nothing is guaranteed. Moving her research and pitch writing to Monday morning meant that Lewis was going to be giving hours she would normally give her best clients to something she didn't have to do. For a diligent person, this time profligacy can feel almost irresponsible.

It is also incredibly effective. Her husband took their kids to school on Mondays so she could get to her desk early. She committed to working on speculative matters from 8:00 A.M. to 10:00 A.M. The result: "Before long, I had written a 900-word pitch, which became a 3,500-word magazine article." This story—called "What If Everything You Knew About Disciplining Kids Was Wrong?"—ran in *Mother Jones* magazine and became the publication's most read piece *ever*. The happy result was that a number of agents expressed interest in representing her. She chose one who seemed compatible, and worked with him to produce a 19,000-word book proposal that multiple publishers bid on. She got her book contract.

In her old schedule, she didn't have time to do the work necessary to build her platform. By investing her peak work hours in this work she wanted to do, she created time. Progress is motivational, and makes time feel expansive. In the time-perception survey, people who strongly agreed with the statement "Yesterday, I made progress toward my personal or professional goals" were 20 percent more likely than the average survey respondent to believe that they generally had enough time for the things they wanted to do.

Time is elastic. It stretches to accommodate what we choose to put into it. Investing in your happiness might mean going for a walk on a beautiful spring morning, even if it means you start work a little later. Generally, the work gets done because it has to get done, but in one world you've started your day with a bit of bliss, while in the normal version of life you haven't. It can mean making space for a hobby or a regular get-together with friends. Even bits of time can be used for bits of joy, like reading via the Kindle app on your phone rather than checking email. You will eventually answer the emails that require answers. You always do. But if there's anything *else* you want to do, happiness comes from doing it first.

Enduring to Enjoying

Investing money and time itself can help make life more enjoyable. But of all the ways to invest in happiness in order to create more time, the most profound is mental.

While your time is, mostly, a choice, parts of life aren't going to be blissful. Sometimes this is because of past choices, or choices made about the future. Sometimes it's pure circumstance. Dark moments are inevitable. On some days, time's eternal ticking can be a blessing. Nothing lasts forever. But if it is possible to flip the switch from enduring to enjoying, or enjoying *while* enduring, this can change the experience of time. To do so one must become, for lack of a better phrase, *good at suffering.*

This is a skill that life sometimes forces people to learn. The blogger known online as Harmony Smith originally wanted to be an attorney. In the process of becoming one, she racked up student loans and credit card debt. She and her husband planned for her to be the primary breadwinner, and they wanted a big family, which they enthusiastically set about producing. Unfortunately, somewhere in this process, Smith realized that she had no stomach for being in the law long term. Hitting her 1,800 billable hours per year made her miserable. And yet with debt and a family to support—a decision to go for a fourth child had the unintended consequence of producing twins—she could not stop working.

But she could make a plan to change her life eventually. She and her husband set a five-year timeline for financial semi-independence: the point at which she could step away from her full-time job and work on a part-time contract basis. (Mr. Smith does part-time projects too, in addition to caring for their five children.) They promised themselves a big reward for meeting their savings goal: they'd take a long RV trip with their brood. And then they embarked on a project of massive frugality and side hustling to achieve this possibility.

That left just one detail: getting through the next five years. Smith's blog, Creating My Kaleidoscope, caught my eye when she published a post calling this stage of life her "five-year prison sentence." That sounds awful, and yet her explanation was not. She was responsible for her debt, and for the fact that it meant she had to work in a highly compensated way. So she was doing her time. And so she told me she was getting through it the same way she imagined she would a real prison sentence:

1. **Know that it is limited.** Five years is five years. It is not forever. It is 1,826 or 1,827 days, depending on how the leap years fall. All time passes, and if you know roughly how long a difficult time will last, you can pace yourself through just about anything.

2. **Take pleasure in what you can.** Sometimes there are things you can enjoy only during times that do not, in themselves, seem enjoyable. But if not, sometimes small good things shine brighter in the middle of darkness. Appreciating them is a mind-set shift that can massively improve your experience of time.

These two coping strategies—these ways of becoming *good at suffering*—are powerful together.

Sometimes, only the first is a possibility. Layla Banihashemi, a neuroscientist whom I began exchanging emails with after she came to one of my speeches, was diagnosed with breast cancer at age thirty-two, four months after her wedding. She endured a long year of chemotherapy, surgery, and radiation. With advances in cancer survival rates, it's easy to forget how awful the treatment can be. Banihashemi found that out soon enough when she had to be hospitalized after her first round of chemotherapy. Lying in her hospital bed, thinking about facing five more rounds and everything that would follow, left her afraid, anxious, overwhelmed. So she got a wall calendar. She wrote out all her treatments for the year. "Somehow, that made it seem more doable," she says. "I will take this day by day for this year."

But sometimes, even day by day was too much. Her suffering took many forms. One round of chemotherapy left her so fatigued she could barely walk from the couch in her living room to the bathroom. She couldn't stand long enough to take a shower. Horribly nauseated after another round, she would lie awake at night unable to sleep. "My husband would sleep on the couch so he wouldn't disturb me, but he would come check on me—every hour, every couple of hours—and sometimes he would say 'just try to make it through the next twenty minutes,'" she says. "That was really helpful. When you're feeling sick, and you think *I'm just trying to make it through the next few minutes,* it brings your focus down to such a narrow place. You're just trying to make it through the moment. You're not thinking about everything else that's to come."

Eventually, a year—even one where you have to count minutes—will be over. She survived, and it was.

If the situation is not so dire, the second strategy can become a possibility. On some days, Banihashemi was able to eat a little more, and go for a walk or do some yoga. She enjoyed these days as she could.

Harmony Smith tries to take this approach of enjoying what she can. She hates saying goodbye to her family in the morning. But not all moments of the five-year "prison sentence" will be bad. Many have been, and will be, nice. Billing 1,800 hours a year might require working 2,500 hours or so, but with 8,760 hours in a year, sleeping 2,920 (eight per night) still leaves 3,340 hours for other things. In that time, "we find creative ways to have fun, enjoy ourselves, and relax without spending money," she says. "We're making the most of it." One December, she went to the library and got two dozen children's Christmas books. She wrapped them up, and the kids got to open a new one each night and read it with her. The family asked for, and received, a zoo membership for one of the children's birthdays, and have enjoyed their outings there.

Sometimes, things that might seem only endurable have some enjoyable aspects to them that are not accessible in different circumstances. Rather than take out a loan to get a van that could accommodate two infant car seats and the older children's seats, Harmony Smith and her husband purchased (and repainted) a used short school bus off Craigslist that they could pay for outright with one year's tax refund. Smith finds people's reactions to her school bus hilarious—and that's a source of laughter she would not have if taking on more debt was an option.

Winter provides another example of this phenomenon. Winter on the East Coast of the United States always seems dark and gloomy to me. But it's nothing compared with the northern parts of Scandinavia, where the polar night stretches from November to well into the new year. Up by the Arctic Circle, the sun does not rise for weeks. Even in the more populated areas in southern Scandinavia, the day is dim and lasts for just a few hours around noon.

It seems improbably depressing, but my husband, who lived in Oslo for five years before we met, reports that it generally isn't to the people who live there. Far-northern types instead view winter as something to be enjoyed, not endured. They eagerly await the start of ski season, skiing being an activity you can do only in winter. They sit in outdoor hot tubs, enjoying the exquisite contrast of a very warm body and a very cold nose. Whatever the weather, they get outside, experiencing the known mood-boosting effects of fresh air. There's a saying that there's no such thing as bad weather, only bad clothing. People light candles and drink hot beverages. Winter festivals cultivate a sense of fun and solidarity. Anyone willing to open his eyes can see that winter can be beautiful. Deep around the solstice, when the sun never completely rises, for multiple hours a day it can look like sunrise or sunset, creating otherworldly luminescence on the snow. It is a different sort of beauty—a harsher, more demanding beauty than a June rose garden—but it is beauty all the same. Because it is all the light you get, you pay attention.

Seeing with New Eyes

This sense of contrast—that what might be missed in normal times can stand out in harsher ones—is a key part of flipping that script from enduring to enjoying. Some people become masters of this special power.

That's the case for Amelia Boone, who is professionally good at suffering. I first saw Boone in a hotel gym in California, where I noticed her defined muscles and that her workout seemed more intense than what the rest of us conference-goers were doing, loping along on the ellipticals. I later learned that this lawyer by day is also a champion obstacle course racer. Like Carneal, she rises before 5:00 A.M. to invest in her happiness; by the time she shows up at work, she may have run twenty miles. This intensity has paid off in her winning the World's Toughest Mudder competition multiple times, becoming the Spartan Race World

Champion in 2013, and placing near the top in several ultra-marathon races (distances longer than 26.2 miles).

She's done many races in tough conditions, but she says the toughest was one of her early ones: the 2011 World's Toughest Mudder competition in Englishtown, New Jersey. It was mid-December, and the temperatures dropped into the teens as people crawled through water and freezing mud under live wires. The course was designed to take about twenty-four hours to finish, so in addition to being exposed to the elements, competitors would be up all night. I tracked down some descriptions from other race participants to try to visualize it. While there were warming tents (and medics) along the route, the course was still miserable. I think the best way to understand it is this: At the starting line, there were close to a thousand obstacle race veterans who'd qualified for this championship by placing high in other races. By sunrise, only about a dozen were left.

Boone was one of them. She got through these torments—and those in all her subsequent competitions—with the same two strategies we talked about earlier.

First, "I pretty much compartmentalize the race." Rather than thinking *I'm two hours in, I have twenty-two to go,* she focuses on getting from obstacle to obstacle, or to the next water stop. "That to me has been the best trick that I've had to help deal with that and to pass the time and not get overwhelmed," she says. She will sing the same song to herself over and over again. You sing it enough, and the time will pass, just as if you count to twenty often enough on a wretchedly turbulent flight, or in the middle of a contraction, or while pounding out a sprint on the treadmill, eventually you will get through.

Yet she doesn't just compartmentalize. Being good at suffering means that even in misery Boone finds things to enjoy. "One of the best ways to pass the time is to engage with your competitors around you. You're moving at a slow enough pace in really long races that you can actually learn about other people and talk," she says. "Some of the people I've met through races have become some of my best friends because you have these shared experiences and memories." Someone who has crawled through freezing mud beside you lands in a different category of relationship than someone who has not. "Feeling pain with other people is a very unifying concept," she says. It is, fortunately, one many of us don't deal with much anymore, but certainly at many times in human history, and in some places now, people suffer through hunger, cold, and disease in groups. That this shared suffering might bring people together rather than turn them against one another is probably why the human race has survived.

Then, there was this pleasure: "The sun coming up is the most glorious moment in those races," she says. That frigid dawn in Englishtown, New Jersey, was the first time Boone had ever run through the night. "It was the coldest I've ever been in my life." Everything hurt—her fingers, her toes—but she was grateful for the hurt because it meant her body was still functional. Then, in that wretched darkness, the first light peeked out over those frozen muddy fields. "I have never felt so euphoric to see the sun," she says. She had survived. She had made it. The sunrise was nothing stunning in the normal sense. Someone out on the road early that Sunday morning would have driven through it thinking nothing. But in the freezing weather, Boone had earned that dawn. That made something normal into something transcendent.

The Discipline of Joy

It is the search for these transcendent moments that keeps many of us muddling through tough times. Grace comes in many forms. Sometimes it is sheer surrender to the possibilities of acceptance. Says Banihashemi, "During one of our middle-of-the-night talks, I remember telling my husband through tears, 'This shouldn't be happening to us.' And he said, 'It is happening. Suffering is part of life.'" She is now on the other side of her year of treatment, and this acceptance has freed her in many ways. She makes time for singing, songwriting, playing the guitar. She spends more time in nature. "One thing that I devote much less time to is worrying about the future," she says. "I think any experience of suffering is worthwhile if you let it change you."

These moments of change or transcendence can appear in all sorts of trying situations. It is that moment in a string of bad first dates when you realize the person across the table from you said something hilarious. That doesn't guarantee love and marriage, but it restores your faith that the process won't all be awful. It can be a late night at the office when you realize that, though the business you're all working for is failing, you admire one of your colleagues enough that you will find some way to work together again. Perhaps the purpose of this line on your résumé was simply to make that moment possible.

Life with little kids features a lot of this muddling pierced with transcendence. The days are long, but there are strategies to make the long days doable, with moments of real happiness. On days I've had whatever number of small kids on my own, I've generally planned a morning outing somewhere pleasant and compatible with the weather: children's museum in the slush, zoo in the sun. We marvel together at the tigers, or the simple bliss of a carousel. We come home around lunch. Then the little ones nap and the big ones get screen or reading time. This provides the supervising adult with about two hours of leisure, and sometimes three if the day goes well. The late-afternoon post-nap slot is good for another activity: an errand, a playground trip. An afternoon playdate is nice too, filling the time until 5:30 P.M. Then it is home to get dinner, get the kids cleaned up and into the most adorable pajamas possible—an aesthetic payoff for wrangling them through the day—and then get the little ones into bed around 7:30 P.M. Get the others to bed in the next ninety minutes. Enjoy more adult downtime until crashing around 10:30 P.M., with the hope that everyone stays down until 6:00 A.M.

It is generally doable enough, but for the first few years of Alex's life, that please-get-me-to-6:00-A.M. request fell on deaf ears. He did not sleep consistently through the night for a long time, and once he did, he'd wake up around 5:00 A.M. many mornings, and for reasonable stretches of time this edged closer to 4:30 A.M.

That might be OK if he had been a docile baby, but he wasn't. He had ambitions to achieve great things before breakfast. He figured out how to climb out of his crib long before his older siblings had managed that trick. We put child locks on the doors, but he'd kick and howl, which meant that even if I ignored him, I couldn't sleep. I remember one morning leaving him for a few minutes in the kitchen so I could go to the bathroom, and when I came back he had climbed up on the counter and dumped an entire jar of fish food in the tank. Our fish did not survive the clean-out. Another morning, when my husband was traveling, I had Alex watch a show on his Kindle so I could shower. I suddenly had a sense that he was no longer in the bathroom. I got out of the shower, ran downstairs, and caught him up on the counter again, just about to pull the full pot of hot coffee out from the coffeemaker and onto himself. I think he was trying to be helpful—*Mommy likes coffee in the morning so I'll get her coffee for her!*—but it was terrifying nonetheless.

So it was hours of early-morning vigilance to fend off fish death and scalding. I could trade off with my husband if he was home, but it felt like my husband found a lot of reasons not to be home, and if the kid was up at 4:30 A.M., the trade-off happened at 6:00 A.M., which still feels early on a Sunday morning. Passing the time during these long, dark mornings involved a lot of watching the clock. Watching the clock is the opposite of being off the clock. It is such a cruel bargain to know your time on earth is limited and yet find yourself wanting the minutes to move faster.

I wish I could write some glib personal essay with a turning point along the lines of "then he hugged me and said 'I love you, Mommy' and it was all worth it!" Life does not conform to a narrative arc. He said "I love you" and it was wonderful, and I was (am) grateful to have a healthy, happy child, but he was up at 4:30 A.M. I would have been grateful for health and happiness if he got up at 6:00 A.M. too. Those mornings were a miserable part of my life for more than two years, requiring me to go to bed long before I wanted in order to hit my 7.4 hours of sleep, and leaving me frazzled by the time I started work.

Yet there were some moments when, contrasted with the general wretchedness of the situation, normal things seemed more profound. When you are exhausted, that first sip of coffee—good coffee: Starbucks dark roast—transports you into the land of the living. I used real cream because 4:45 A.M. is no time for skim milk. Unlike Boone, I hadn't been out in the freezing cold all night, but when you've been up for hours already, seeing the sunrise can be its own moment of beauty. I recall one morning on vacation at Rehoboth Beach, when Alex was up at 4:30 A.M., and I took the stroller out to see that fiery sun pop up over the Atlantic. The sky was as pink and orange as sherbet in the boardwalk ice-cream parlors. There were long periods of my adult life when I was never up for the sunrise, so seeing those bright streaks was a prize that was possible due only to my son's insomnia. I celebrated small milestones, like when he became interested enough in TV to reliably sit for ten minutes. As for investing in my happiness, I sometimes structured my business trips not to take the red-eye home. I'd stay over to fly during the day, and sleep undisturbed in my hotel room for one more night.

These things helped, but my most important discovery was this: joy is a discipline. We may lament the Hemingway quote that starts this chapter—that happiness in intelligent people is rare—but he is not wrong. Thoughtful people naturally construct stories to make sense of their lives. It takes real work to keep one unpleasant aspect of your life from becoming your entire narrative. Many intelligent people can't muster themselves to do this work; hence, the tendency to brood.

As a veteran parent I knew things would get better eventually with my son, and slowly they have. But viewing those first few years of his life as a time for hanging on would have been a mistake. So many other wonderful things happened alongside these woes. I could be miserably roused from sleep at 4:30 A.M. and yet later that day feel on top of the world after taking my big kids to an arcade and landing on the leaderboard for a game. I could be up at 4:30 A.M. and yet enjoy a lovely hour reading on the porch as the sun set at night.

The discipline of joy requires holding in the mind simultaneously that this too shall pass and that this too is *good*. This alchemy of mind isn't easy, but the good life is not always the easy life. Happiness requires effort. It is not just bestowed; it is the earned interest on what you choose to pay in.

SIX

LET IT GO

Dripping water hollows out stone.
—Ovid, *Epistulae ex Ponto* IV

From time to time on my blog, I offer "time makeovers" to people who are willing to let me write about them. Laureen Marchand, a sixty-six-year-old Canadian artist who lives in Saskatchewan, wrote me in the summer of 2016 that she thought she could use some help. She told me that she was "not as productive" as she wanted to be, and in the beginning of our correspondence, she seemed to be looking for standard advice on getting more done. She noted that she was frequently distracted from her creative work. Her one-week time log showed that she was working forty-one hours at her various commitments, including supervising an artist residency program, dealing with administrative matters, and working part-time at a local grocery store. Only twelve of these work hours, however, were spent on her top priority of making art.

She wanted this ratio to change, so I gave some advice from the previous chapter: pay yourself first. When you are combining creative, speculative work with professional activities, if you wait until the end of the day or the end of the week to make art, there may not be time left over. But if you carve out time on Monday morning for such work—as Katherine Reynolds Lewis did with her pitching—it will get done.

Marchand thought this sounded sensible. She would aim to make it to the studio on Monday by 9:30 A.M., and on any other day that wasn't committed as well.

A while later, however, she wrote back to tell me that she had just experienced an incredibly frustrating week. She was also realizing some things about her life and work that she wanted to share with me.

Marchand, I learned, had built an impressive artistic career over the prior decades, exhibiting in more than two dozen solo and two-person shows, and in forty group shows. You might think this describes a cosmopolitan artist, but in fact she lives "literally in the middle of nowhere." Her village of Val Marie has about 130 people. The nearest substantial town is seventy-five miles away. The area, right by Canada's Grasslands National Park, is ruggedly beautiful enough to justify the artist residency program she supervised at the time, and she is well plugged in to her small community (the grocery store gig was as much about seeing her neighbors as anything else). The remoteness, however, has drawbacks. She needed to drive long distances when she had a doctor appointment, or needed to pick up supplies. If she needed service people to come to her house, she was truly at their mercy because they would only come to Val Marie when they wanted to come to Val Marie.

"I'm glad I moved here because I love the landscape and the lower cost of living," she told me. But "it does add a layer of difficulty to managing an artistic career, especially as I'm 66 and my energy is not getting greater every year."

Logistical issues are what they are, but on top of that, "earlier this year I had what I now recognize was a burnout and a creative block at the same time. I'm still working my way back from those," she said. "I'm a slow producer at the best of times, and this definitely wasn't the best."

So that was the background for the annoying week that followed her original log, in which she "had every kind of interruption—medical, job-related, contract-related, plumbing. I agree completely about spending the best time of the day on the most important thing, so on Monday morning I made a list of all the other tasks that were calling, which enabled me to put them off for later, and I got almost six studio hours."

Unfortunately, though, "this was the last time in the week that happened."

Tuesday she drove seventy miles round-trip to a rural health clinic for a fasting blood test. Some complication occurred in this, and so "that turned into another trip of the same distance the next morning, Wednesday, for the same thing." Later on Wednesday morning, the plumber came to install a new water pump on her well, and the latest resident artist left. "I did manage some studio time in each afternoon, but it was less than I wanted. Thursday was my job day"—that is, the grocery store gig—"which instead of being just the morning, lasted six hours due to the temporary staff shortage. Friday I felt just drained and was incapable of getting going in the studio until after noon."

The fun went on. "Now the new water pump isn't working properly, which means my water supply is uncertain." She was facing another plumber visit, whenever that would be. In her ideal world, she said, "I would make art between 9:00 A.M. and 4:00 P.M. five days a week and go for a walk after that. In the real world, it's 90 degrees by 4:00 P.M. this time of year, the plumbing and lights quit, and every project seems to take longer and be more demanding than I thought it would be."

I looked at her log, and had a few thoughts about batching errands—key, if you have to drive seventy miles—but I noted something important: She had been in the studio working on art for 16.5 hours during this difficult week. This was more than the twelve hours she had done during the previous week she sent me. She was getting to the studio, and she was increasing her hours there. That should be celebrated. The only problem was her expectation for something different. Her frustration about this—more than individual house woes or doctor trips—was likely hindering her creativity.

So I wrote this: "Another way to think of this is just to be gentle on yourself. You're coming out of quite a burnout, as you said, and sometimes that requires time and space. If you managed 16.5 hours on art, that's much better than the zero that often accompanies a creative block."

She could commit to paying herself first, but she could also repeat this mantra: *Make art when you can. Relax when you can't.*

She decided to try this perspective. She kept up with the Monday routine, making sure to preserve that time for art. Then, instead of feeling guilty when she wasn't in the studio, she scheduled some major self-care: coffee with friends, a Saturday-night dinner.

The effect was liberating. Despite entertaining a plumber for an entire morning—and learning that she'd need to have a new well put in—"it feels like I had a holiday." That was "because I wasn't trying to squeeze out art time when there was none to squeeze." Looking ahead to the next week, she wrote, "I should have at least two of Wednesday, Friday, and Saturday this week for art days. And I'll try to take them for what they are." If she could not work, it was fine. If she could, that was great.

This liberation from expectations turned out to be helpful during the next week, which was equally challenging. Her water system almost completely gave out, so she had to take laundry to a friend's house, take one-minute showers, and water her garden with a can. "So I was glad to make art when I could, and give myself permission not to on days when I was too tired or there was too much going on," she says. She made it to the studio four days, generally in the morning. "And on all the days art happened, I was very glad of it. It felt great. And I think it felt great partly because I knew I could relax with what was possible on the other days. I would still like more art days but can cut myself some slack when it isn't possible."

When she stopped beating herself up about her lack of output, Marchand turned out to be quite productive. She made good use of her time in the studio, working on her oil paintings of flowers. These still-life works explored how light would play on the petals, the glass vases, the water. A few weeks later she wrote me, "Yesterday I finished the first painting I've completed since April, and now I'm planning the next one." It became the next entry in what soon became a botanical series. "I'll have an image of the finished piece on my website later today," she said. "I wondered if this day would ever come."

The Wages of Expectations

While I am not living in rural Saskatchewan, I sympathize with Marchand's original frustration. A recent week's litany of domestic distractions: We had plumbers out on two different days to diagnose a problem with our sewage ejector system, which is one of those expensive and completely unsexy home-ownership woes that no one ever wants to spend time and money on. Ruth had a school tour scheduled for a half-day kindergarten enrichment program. She also had a follow-up doctor visit after she failed her hearing test at her well-child visit due to an ear infection.

All of this could, of course, be spun toward gratitude. Her hearing is fine! We live near good school programs! I can afford home improvements! Still, as I wound up bringing all four children to Jasper's karate class on Tuesday afternoon because of scheduling snafus stemming from our minivan needing to be dropped off at a repair shop, I recalled that some authors in their book acknowledgments thank their families for putting up with their absences for months as they wrote. I pictured these writers so secluded in their garrets that they later needed to apologize for all those missed dinners.

Somehow, my life did not seem to be structured that way.

It is tempting to give in to gloom about these things. While I try not to fill time, sometimes time gets filled anyway. I find myself in the midst of a busy week with just one morning completely open and ninety-minute chunks of open time elsewhere. But then a funny thing happens. When I tell myself *OK, you only have this time, just do what you can do,* I surprise myself. I can write an article draft in a few hours. I can edit it in those ninety-minute chunks. Indeed, when I tell myself to just do what I can, even if it is only a little bit, because it is better than nothing, that something, done repeatedly, adds up.

We all have the same amount of time, so feeling like we have all the time in the world is really about managing expectations. Some suffering—the kind we must learn to be good at—is inevitable. But other suffering is self-imposed. In particular, we suffer when expectations exceed reality. This suffering is a major cause of wasted time. Mental anguish and rumination eat up hours. They also keep us from enjoying the time we have. The internet is full of fake Buddha quotes, but I like this real one from the *Dhammapada:*

> *If you are filled with desire*
> *Your sorrows swell*
> *Like the grass after the rain.*
> *But if you subdue desire*
> *Your sorrows shall fall from you*
> *Like drops of water from a lotus flower.*

Being able to let go of unrealistic expectations can make us feel more relaxed about time. Here, though, is where the magic happens: I really do believe that, paradoxically, low expectations in the short run, if met consistently, are what lead to great things in the long run. A one-year-old child babbles. A three-year-old can have a full conversation. That two-year gap is bridged not by hours of forced language drills and berating the child for her slow progress, but by daily praise of every new word and linguistic discovery. To paraphrase another wise man's drops of water reference, little drips hollow the stone. This happens not by force, but by *persistence.*

Make art when you can. Relax when you can't. Good enough is good enough. It is not an excuse for laziness. Letting go of expectations is perfectly compatible with working long hours when that is possible, but when it comes to creative achievement, and when it comes to a truly enjoyed life, being gentle—*persistently gentle*—is just as likely to coax out good outcomes as anything else.

Forget the Best

This chapter is about learning to free up time by letting go of problematic expectations. These come in many forms, generally pertaining to decisions, goals, and relationships.

For many people, the first category—decision making—is a major source of angst. Certain personalities are more prone to decision-making angst than others. In the taxonomy of Barry Schwartz, currently a professor at the University of California, Berkeley, and the author of *The Paradox of Choice*, people are "maximizers" or "satisficers":

- Maximizers want the absolute best option.

- Satisficers have a set of criteria, and go for the first option that clears the bar.

Wanting the best seems like a positive character trait. My children shout such mantras in karate class: "I'm on a quest to be the best!" No one is going to build a career as a motivational speaker by announcing, "I settle! I settle all the time!"

Yet Schwartz's research finds that satisficers tend to be happier than maximizers because they don't waste time ruminating over choices and expectations. People who want the best tend to be prone to regret when their choices turn out not to be perfect in some way. "If you're out to find the best possible job, no matter how good it is, if you have a bad day, you think there's got to be something better out there," Schwartz told me when I interviewed him for a *Fast Company* story in 2016. A bad day can't be accepted as a bad day. It becomes evidence of some larger narrative of life being on the wrong track.

People who want the best are also prone to measuring themselves against others. "If you're looking for the best, social comparison is inevitable," Schwartz told me. "There's no other way to know what the best is." Your house can be the best house only if it is better than everyone else's house. That means you have to look at everyone else's house, and in a world of 7 billion people, or even among the 468 people you follow on Instagram, someone's house is bound to be nicer. Envy leads to misery. As novelist and essayist Joseph Epstein once wrote, "Of the seven deadly sins, only envy is no fun at all."

Satisficers, on the other hand, know that "the idea of the best is preposterous," Schwartz told me. "There is no best anything." Platonic ideals don't exist in the real world; they exist only in those books you haven't opened since your ancient-philosophy class in college. In the real world we also deal with the limitations of money, time, and physics. Even if there were a best house, it wouldn't be in your budget.

Satisficers approach decisions with a list of important criteria, like how close the house is to work, how much redecorating its kitchen needs, and how many bathrooms it has. The criteria don't have to be noble; if it's important to you that a house look impressive enough to wow relatives, so it goes.

But then know this: anything that satisfies your important

criteria will be fine. Good enough is almost always good enough. While the "best" house no longer makes you happy when someone else's house is better, a house chosen because it is close to work, has four bedrooms, and sports front yard landscaping that makes you smile when you pull in the driveway will still do all these things regardless of what a friend's house is like.

If this is true of houses, it's probably true of romantic choices too, though that is even harder for people to get their heads around. The romantic ideal has no place for settling. Yet if you think about it, unless you are the Platonic ideal of a spouse, you're really trying to find the best person who is willing to settle for *you*. Love glows strong in its early stages of newness and uncertainty. After the dust settles, the inevitable fights about money, child raising, and the sewage ejector system might lead a maximizer to believe she married the wrong person. But a satisficer knows that everyone marries the wrong person in the sense that there is no "right" person. Every relationship takes effort. As philosopher (and novelist) Alain de Botton once wrote, "Choosing whom to commit ourselves to is merely a case of identifying which particular variety of suffering we would most like to sacrifice ourselves for." You survey your options for suffering, go with someone of good character, to whom you are sexually attracted, and then, barring disaster, commit to making it work. That is the real road to happily ever after.

Happiness is a great reason to let good enough be good enough, but for our purposes, it is important to note that satisficing saves incredible quantities of time.

My husband and I are both total satisficers. We scheduled our wedding to take place about six months after we got engaged, which I later learned is considered a swift turnaround. But I was fine with choosing a dress on the first day of looking, and I just picked a florist in town who had good reviews and told him to run with it. Putting off getting married for another year to spend more time deliberating on cake decoration seemed insane.

We've continued with this theme in our married life. Here's how we chose a preschool after we moved to Pennsylvania: Some friends sent their kid to a place close to our new house, and liked it. We figured we would too. This mind-set can also help with making decisions about consumer items. If your sister-in-law has a similar life to yours and is happy with her car, you will probably be happy with that same model. This is exactly how I wound up driving an Acura MDX. You could spend weeks researching a cell phone plan, or you could call a friend who just chose one and go with what she chose. If I am at a business lunch, I'll either order the chicken Caesar salad (most restaurants seem to have one) or ask the waiter what he likes. That way, I can focus on my companion, not the menu.

Given how much time that satisficing saves, it raises this question: Is it possible for a maximizer to become a satisficer? I mentioned my restaurant habit to a more maximizing acquaintance, whose wide-eyed reaction was telling: What if the waiter is just trying to push a certain dish the kitchen wants to move? My satisficer self found this ridiculous. Even if he was, so what?

It is not my last supper. It may not even be my last meal at that restaurant. Next time I'll order something else. This is not a decision to get worked up about—but to a maximizer, of course, decisions *are* something to get worked up about.

Schwartz told me he thinks it's possible, if not easy, to learn satisficing. People exist along a continuum, and no one is a maximizer about everything. Someone who spends months agonizing about the "best" car may be fine with whatever garbage bags are on sale.

So if you have read the past few paragraphs and recognize yourself as a maximizer, know this: You don't need to learn an entirely new skill. You're simply transferring an existing skill from one domain to others where it might save you more time. When the maximizing habit kicks in during a medium-stakes situation (for example, you're choosing a hotel for next month's long weekend getaway), just pick something that a friend mentioned or a chain that you've stayed with before. Then, after you've stayed there, ask yourself if you noticed significant downsides. You probably didn't. Most hotels do a decent job of housing people. Most restaurants do a decent job of feeding people. Most suitcases do a decent job of protecting their contents.

If you find yourself feeling miserable as you compare your choices with other people's, then don't put yourself in a place where you see other people's choices. There are many reasons to get off social media. Becoming happy with "good enough" is as good of one as any.

Some reformed maximizers tell me they respond well to

time pressure, or to taking themselves out of the equation. Shelley Young, who works in marketing in the restaurant industry, told me that she had endured various problems in her old house for a long time. "I didn't want to make a mistake on a big investment that I would have to live with for years," she said. But when she decided to put the house on the market, she suddenly had to fix those problems. Because she wouldn't be living there, she was "able to make fast decisions about everything, just going with what was most neutral." Turns out, her design instincts were pretty good. "It was beautiful, but we only enjoyed it for three months until we moved out." In her new home, she made sure to get the decisions made quickly so she could actually enjoy her place.

Likewise, if you find yourself dithering over something, a deadline can help. Give yourself five minutes to choose a restaurant. You could even pretend you're sending a recommendation to a group of people you don't know all that well. When the alarm goes off, go with the best option you've found. Then, reward yourself for your efficiency. If you took five minutes to decide on lunch rather than an hour, you can use the saved time to stay for dessert.

"Better Than Nothing" Goals

The second domain in which problematic expectations cause time-wasting anguish is goals. I write about productivity; it would be sacrilege to disavow goals. So I won't. Setting long-term directions can help orient the present and sometimes help people survive unpleasant presents.

But I think the way people set goals is often counterproductive. The temptation is to focus on outcomes: losing fifteen pounds, or reaching $1 million in business revenue. On the way to the outcome, there can be ups and downs, which can be discouraging, even though many of these ups and downs cannot be controlled. So people waste time obsessing about the numbers.

Better to focus on process goals, which are habits by a different name. These are within your control, and when done regularly tend to lead toward the desired outcome over time. Indeed, they often lead toward the outcome in a better way than simply focusing on the outcome (which has a tendency to encourage shortcuts, if you believe the headlines on bank employees fudging numbers to collect their bonuses).

Someone who might normally resolve to lose fifteen pounds, for example, could instead decide to exercise daily, drink water instead of sugar-sweetened beverages, eat vegetables at lunch and dinner, and not snack after 8:30 P.M. Someone trying to grow a business might resolve to pursue five new leads per week, and reach out to former clients once a quarter.

Angst with goals comes from fear of failure. But if you focus on process, then what might be perceived as failure when looking at outcomes isn't really failure.

As a goal junkie, I have to remind myself of this. I set a goal for the first quarter of 2016—shared publicly on my blog—to make it through an eighteen-minute speed workout I'd clipped from *Oxygen* magazine. I got close, but I never made it through the entire progressive session of two minutes at 6.0 mph, two minutes at 7.0 mph, two minutes at 8.0 mph, and two minutes at 9.0 mph. I'd gotten to ninety seconds at 9.0 mph and had pretty much fallen off the treadmill.

I was lamenting this as I was interviewing a goal expert when he reminded me that I had pulled that number out of the air. There was nothing magical about the *Oxygen* workout. What was true was that I was faster on March 31 than I was on January 1. In the course of throwing myself at that speed workout, I'd done many things I didn't think I could do before. I had run a sub-eight-minute mile. I had done short sprints at 10.0 mph. Thinking of myself as a failure discounted the hard work I'd done. Focusing on the work itself might have been smarter. Any day I'd done my sprints, I'd know I'd made progress. Small steps lead to big things over time.

Indeed, if you want to sustain a habit over time, I'd recommend making the process goals as doable as possible. Make them small to the point where you feel no resistance to meeting them. Set them so you can exceed them with ego-boosting regularity. These little goals are simply "better than nothing." As a friend noted to me, we could call them BTN goals.

Streaks—those longest lasting of habits—are all about BTN goals. I have long been fascinated by people who do something daily for decades. That's probably because my father is one of these people. In the summer of 1977, when he was a thirty-one-year-old professor of religion at North Carolina State University, he decided that he should read more Hebrew. He already taught the language and studied ancient biblical texts, so he wanted to build language practice into his life. He began reading Hebrew for thirty minutes per day. He continued to do this for the next four decades. He tells me that there was one day in the 1980s when he read for about ten minutes and then got distracted, and then the day was over. But other than that, the streak is perfect. He read Hebrew on the days my little brother and I were born. He even managed to read on the two days he had eye surgery. He stayed up until midnight the night before to read, and then by the end of the second day after surgery, he was recovered enough to do his reading.

I inherited aspects of my father's personality, though up until 2017 I had never consciously tried a streak. I say "consciously" because, as I think about it, I am on a multidecade streak of brushing my teeth daily. I am pretty sure I have eaten and slept at some point in any given twenty-four-hour period as far back as I can recall. It is quite possible to avoid doing any of these things for a twenty-four-hour period, but life simply feels better when I do them. People with long-running streaks tend to feel the same way about their habits.

Reading Hebrew wouldn't do much for me, but I do love to run, and to set running goals, if some are more useful than others. So over the holidays in late 2016, nine months after missing my progressive-speed workout goal, I decided to try something different: I would start a running streak. I would challenge myself to run at least a mile every day. A mile is a BTN distance, nothing much on its own, but I thought I'd see how it went.

The BTN aspect turned out to be effective in getting me to run more. I did not feel like running every day, but it was only a mile. That usually takes me less than ten minutes. Even on my worst, slowest, nose-is-stuffy-and-the-baby-was-up-early days, I could shuffle through twelve minutes of 5.0 mph forward motion. Because I knew I could quit after twelve minutes, I would just go ahead and run it. But in running, the first mile is usually the hardest. By the time I'd run a mile, I felt fine to keep going. I didn't have to. I simply could if I wanted to. And often I did.

My running streak changed the conversation I had with myself. The question wasn't *if* I would run, it was *when* I would run. This was simply a matter of thinking through the schedule. It turned out that, if the question was *when*, most circumstances allowed for a short run. After preserving the streak through some early hiccups (for example, a stomach bug; I'd had the foresight to run *before* I started vomiting one day, and then, as with my father's surgeries, by the end of the second day, I was OK to do a little something), I realized it was within my power to continue it. So I did. Even if it meant running laps in a hotel room because it was snowing and the hotel gym treadmill was unavailable. Thirty days turned to sixty, then a hundred, then three hundred, and so on.

I don't want to make too much of this, because I know the streak will end, possibly before this book hits shelves, and certainly before the four decades my father has achieved. I also know myself. I know I am subject to a "tightening" impulse that can make the habit the master, not me, or at least account for some curious quirks. At some point, I started running 1.1 miles—not 1.0 miles—on my BTN days to cover any inadvertent walking that occurred while I was starting up the treadmill.

That said, there is a lesson here. Looking at my running logs, I can see that I have often been running at least a 5K (3.1 miles) daily through the streak. If I'd set that as a goal—run a 5K daily!—I wouldn't have lasted long. It would be too much for those days when I really could run only a mile. Lowering expectations to the point of no resistance is what makes bigger things possible.

The Secret of Prolificacy

As I study prolific people who seem relaxed and yet get so much done, I see that this is often their secret: small things done repeatedly add up. You do not have to work around the clock. You simply put one metaphorical foot in front of the other, achieve your small goal, then do it again. If you do this often enough, you can fit seemingly impossible things into your life.

Katy Cannon, a UK-based novelist, reports that she has developed this more persistent and abundant perspective on time over the years. At the start of 2013, she had a four-year-old daughter and had just sold her first book. Her contract called for her to turn in another book six months later, which seemed like the sort of work/life disaster one might need to write a very British novel about. But she did it, and in 2016 she wrote and edited five books, a novella, and three short stories (also using the pen name Sophie Pembroke).

This is how she makes such prolificacy work. She takes about two weeks to plan her books, outlining scenes and working with her editors on characters and plots. Then, execution happens in small bursts. She sets a timer, and in a twenty- to thirty-minute block of total focus, she can write an 800- to 1,000-word scene. She does two or three of these blocks a day, generally putting down 2,000 to 3,000 words.

This is not a huge number; I suspect the average office worker cranks out close to 2,000 words in emails daily. But 2,000 is enough, because Cannon just keeps going. Over a four-day workweek of these two or three bursts per day, she produces about 10,000 words. That means she can write a 70,000- to 80,000-word novel draft in seven to eight weeks. Add in the planning time and two weeks for editing, and that's a full book in eleven to twelve weeks.

Are the books perfect? No, but no book is ever perfect, even ones that take eleven to twelve years to write. As for some idealized book that never made it out of the author's head, where it would be sullied by reality? We don't even need to have this conversation. Cannon's books have the virtue of being completed and out in the world, giving readers pleasure. *Done is better than perfect, because there is no perfect without being done.*

Some of this speed is practical: "I don't have time to sit around and wait for the muse, because I've got bills to pay!" she says.

But some is also experience, and regular writing generates its own virtuous cycle. The more books she writes, the more book ideas she gets. That means she's ready to write the next book as soon as the previous one is on its way into production. The more books she writes, the more efficient she becomes. "I see problems before they happen," she says. "I don't write as much of the stuff that won't work later." The more books she writes, the deeper her stories turn out to be. "Each of my characters does enough to justify her place in the story from the start. Each of my scenes is working harder. They're doing two or three things." With persistence, the more things fit right the first time. So she does not need to second-guess herself. She can avoid the mental anguish that keeps people from typing the 800 words necessary to introduce a secondary character to the narrator and foreshadow an argument two other characters will have later. There is time to write the scene, and time later to make it better. Neither need take years. "The sort of time you think is required generally isn't," she says. "There's a point of diminishing returns."

Love Is Acceptance

The last category where letting go of expectations can reduce anguish and free up space is relationships with people. This includes ourselves.

In general, people are a good use of time—a subject we'll return to in the next chapter—but people have to be taken as they are. People do change, but only because they decide they want to change, not because someone else has spent enough time worrying about it.

Parenting in particular is one long lesson in letting go of expectations. This begins early on, when that nursery that looked so great on Pinterest is rearranged to accommodate the need to strip soiled sheets at 2:00 A.M. The notion that children are inherently peaceful bangs into the discovery that your toddler is the one biting everyone at day care. Family dinner does not happen every night. When it does, it might involve a lot of chicken nuggets. The kids will watch too much TV. They will get bad grades on the occasional test, and if they don't, that doesn't mean all is great either. An unchallenged kid might be hopelessly bored and plotting subterfuge. All will not go well. You will spend big bucks to go to Disney World and your child will refuse to leave the hotel pool.

You can spend much time wanting your children to be different. You can make progress on certain things, such as table manners and enforced teeth brushing. But ultimately children are their own people. Detached from any expectation of who they should be, they often turn out to be very cool little people. There is much time saved and, more important, *pleasure* in acceptance: in getting to know them as they are.

I also believe in getting to know ourselves as we are, and being gentle, as we would with any other friend we've known since childhood. It is in this space of letting go of expectations where progress is possible. When I get frustrated with my writing, I like to read the words Ernest Hemingway used to assure himself in *A Moveable Feast:* "Do not worry. You have always written before and you will write now. All you have to do is write one true sentence. Write the truest sentence that you know." What writer minds writing one sentence? A paragraph here, a paragraph there. The words that need to come out will come out with gentle persistence. Love, including self-love, is patient, which is really another word for being generous with time.

As for Laureen Marchand, over the next year she embraced this mental shift for herself. "Your idea of 'make art when you can' made quite a difference to me," she says. "It helped me realize that being stressed when I wasn't able to be in my studio wasn't making anything better; it was reducing the energy I did have to use during the time available." But then there was this: "It also helped me see that the feelings art-making engenders are more valuable than anything created by my other commitments."

When art felt good rather than stressful, she discovered that she really did want to do more art. She wanted to make it her top priority in life.

So she took a leave of absence from her supermarket job. She bequeathed much of her volunteer work to other people. Then she signed on to do an exhibition of her light-flooded botanical paintings in March 2017, and doubled down on her time in the studio. She completed three paintings in 2016, then ramped up her pace to complete five in the first two months of 2017.

This was intense. She reported to her studio almost every day. She finished the last painting at 3:00 P.M. on the Tuesday before her Saturday opening. She delivered it to the gallery on Friday. "Being as they're oil paintings and take a while to dry, it was too soft even to put a plastic bag around it," she says. But the show went well, with "excellent attendance" and sales too.

She was proud of all she had done. Putting painting first had been exhilarating, but she was still gentle with herself about the time she had spent not painting. "It surprises me a bit to know that I don't blame myself for not making that decision earlier," she says. "If I could have, I would have. And when I could, I did." There were trade-offs; for one thing, she missed seeing her neighbors through the grocery store job. "But I'll find some other form of connection that doesn't cause such fatigue," she says. "This taste of pure artist life has taken away any taste at all for other people's schedules."

SEVEN

PEOPLE ARE A GOOD USE OF TIME

What is your friend that you should seek him with hours to kill? Seek him always with hours to live.

—Kahlil Gibran, *The Prophet*

When I arranged a joint phone interview with Elisabeth McKetta and Cathy Doggett for a *Fast Company* story on friendship a few years ago, I wrote up a long list of questions to ask. That is always my strategy for such things; when there's a lull, I move to the next item. But as soon as these best friends started talking, I realized that I didn't need to do anything to get the stories flowing. I was stepping into a conversation that had been going on for decades. They laughed as a single word triggered shared memories. They finished each other's sentences.

Their mothers—who knew each other in Texas—had encouraged them to meet when they were both in their twenties and living in Boston. They discovered that they were both vegetarians and liked to cook. Doggett was the more organized, mature one;

she suggested they meet every Monday to cook dinner. She always had recipes picked, and "there was always wine," notes McKetta.

When they moved to separate cities because of jobs and families—McKetta now lives in Boise, Idaho, and Doggett in Austin, Texas—they continued to speak to each other by phone, even though neither particularly likes this form of communication. Indeed, Doggett told me she speaks more with McKetta than she does with anyone who lives closer by. It's not just chitchat. They talk deliberately about their lives. They discuss their goals and progress toward them. They discuss books they've decided to read together.

When I followed up later, after my story appeared, I learned that their relationship has had its bumps, as all long relationships do. "She holds very high expectations of all the people in her life," says McKetta of Doggett. "I've always naturally been a little flakier." She has forgotten to return phone calls. She once rented out her Boise house to a jazz band when Doggett was scheduled to visit.

These divergent personalities led to one of their first clashes, though McKetta now recalls it as a favorite foundational memory. They'd planned their Monday dinner, but then McKetta suggested shortly before the get-together that she might go hear a visiting speaker that evening. Doggett would be fine if they moved dinner to some other day, right? "She very sternly said, 'No. No we may not. I have made this plan for you. I have the food, and it's not going to be good by Wednesday. You don't have to do it, but I'm not going to be able to reschedule.'" It was an eye-opening moment for McKetta. "She held me accountable," she says.

But lest you think Doggett is completely inflexible, she's not. It was more that she was encouraging McKetta to be respectful of her time, setting ground rules for a relationship that could continue for decades. She knew that if McKetta was constantly breaking and stringing along plans, she wouldn't feel strongly about continuing the friendship. She wanted to continue the friendship, so she would not let her out of her agreements as easily as someone she didn't care for. "I felt chosen and excited to rise to the challenge," says McKetta. "She's very good at asking questions that show a long, deep concern for my well-being."

They'd talk about how each might build a satisfying life. Doggett has encouraged McKetta to be more focused. McKetta helps Doggett relax, occasionally doing such things as looking at Doggett's extensive meal plans and asking *why* she is planning dinner more than a few days in advance. Their friendship helps both of them see the world in a different way. And over time it creates its own weight: "She's been a witness to every single one of my adult evolutions," says McKetta. A disagreement with a colleague can be put in perspective. They've both seen it all before. "It's so freeing to get to keep living and sharing it all with her."

Or as Doggett puts it, sharing ups and downs "has made life less lonely and more meaningful."

This life enrichment is the point of having friends. "Let there be no purpose in friendship save the deepening of the spirit," writes Kahlil Gibran in that graduation gift of a volume known as *The Prophet*. Most people crave the sort of deep relationship that Doggett and McKetta have. While some people are fortunate enough to have this kind of relationship with a spouse or a sibling, we recognize that building such soulfulness into other relationships would make life better in many ways. Time spent in communion with our closest companions is among the most truly off-the-clock sensations we have. Indeed, when people express their misgivings about the whole concept of time management to me, they generally present a structured approach to time as being incompatible with long, leisurely hours spent with much-loved family and friends.

I understand this thinking. I love afternoons that stretch into evenings as I sit in a friend's kitchen chatting about life. I also think such objections miss the point. In a distracted world, you have to decide to make relationships a priority. When I spoke with McKetta alone, she told me that her decades-long friendship with Doggett happened because Doggett "chose me with that kind of organized persistence." Doggett made time in her life for McKetta, and committed to keep doing so, and committed to holding McKetta to that same expectation. When McKetta wavered, she was willing to talk and get issues out in the open.

This requires incredible mindfulness. It requires deciding, in a busy life, to give people the attention they deserve. That is a splendid choice; in general, people are an excellent use of time. Unfortunately, it is a difficult choice amid work and family demands. Without conscious intervention, nurturing relationships will almost automatically fall to the bottom of the to-do list. Friends drift apart; people living in Boise and Austin are never going to accidentally bump into one another. Couples become roommates. Professional collegiality becomes a transactional thing, done to the extent it must be. Even children, who by their nature consume much time, get time that doesn't feel like it is deepening anyone's spirit. We dream of transcendence but live in the reality of making sure everyone's permission slips get back to school on time.

True time masters know that some days will feel like a slog. Still, you can increase the odds of off-the-clock moments in your relationships through careful planning and smart rituals. You can also change the perception of certain moments into more meaningful moments by repeating the mantra that people are worth the bother. They don't just help pass the time. They can make hours come alive.

People Expand Time

This chapter is about how to create more space in your life for close relationships, and make good choices for what you do within that space. Doing these things can increase the happiness in your life, and can make you feel like you have more time. In my survey, people's time-perception scores rose in direct proportion to time spent with friends and family during that March Monday. While the average survey taker's log showed seventy-two minutes actively spent with friends and family, people in the top 20 percent of time-perception scores spent ninety-six minutes, and people in the bottom spent fifty-two minutes. Again, it wasn't that the people on the bottom of the scale had less time than anyone else. I believe the equation goes in the opposite direction: time with friends and loved ones tends to feel relaxed, and good, and hence makes you feel like you have more time. Time spent perusing Twitter does not.

I particularly saw this when I studied the time logs of people in the top 3 percent of time-perception scores. Their language was different from those in the bottom 3 percent. It was more inclusive: "walk/run with kids and dog," "visit sick friend," "ate dinner with my whole family," "talked to spouse and ate dinner," "wife and I do our Monday-evening chores." Even in normal activities, people with high time-perception scores were engaged with the people they wished to have in their lives, whereas those with lower time-perception scores were more likely not to include these engagements, even though other people clearly lived in the same house.

People who strongly agreed that they had made time the day before for people who were important to them were 15 percent more likely than average to say they generally had time for the things they wanted to do. If you take the long view, making time for people can literally increase how much time you have. People with tight social ties tend to live longer and maintain better health than people without such ties. Some of this is surely correlative. Healthy people are more likely to get married, and they have the energy to visit friends and family, but there's evidence for causation too. Friends and family members make you feel less stressed, they urge you to take better care of yourself, and they take care of you and encourage you when you are sick. The result is that, in terms of longevity, having close relationships is roughly akin to quitting smoking.

Plan for Relationships

So how do people who make time for people structure their hours to deepen their spirits? How do they build lives that allow them to enjoy this time enough to feel off the clock?

As Gibran's prophet instructs the people of the town he is leaving, "What is your friend that you should seek him with hours to kill? Seek him always with hours to live." The wisdom in this is the recognition that people tend to allocate the nurturing of their relationships to whatever time is left over once the have-to-dos are done. *If* I can get this report done by mid-afternoon, *then* I'll ask the new hire to grab coffee with me. I'll call my friend once I've gotten through all these emails. I'll ask my spouse about that thing I know is bothering her *after* we've gotten the kids to bed and picked up the house. The predictable flaw in this plan is that during the busy years of building a career and raising a family, it can feel like there isn't a whole lot of time there for the killing. Any free hours tend to come at our lowest energy times, which makes it tempting to spend those hours on the effortless fun of TV and social media rather than on something more demanding.

People who make time for people avoid this trap by doing just what Gibran suggests. They "seek him always with hours to live" by treating relationships with the same intentionality as that ultimate have-to-do: work.

While people do plenty of inefficient things in the contexts of their jobs, one reason "work" seems to take more mental space than the hours alone suggest is that people think about where they'd like to be going in their work and what it might take to get there. They think about when they might do those things. Very few people treat their relationships—particularly personal relationships—with anything approaching this intentionality. This is true even if the hours might be similar (my time logs will often show me working forty hours and spending forty combined hours with my kids and husband over the course of a week). Some super-parent sorts might treat their children's talent development with this intentionality, but that's more of a coaching/managerial mind-set. It's not about the growth of the relationship itself.

Treating relationships with the same intentionality as work doesn't mean scheduling family time on weekends in fifteen-minute blocks, or sending calendar invites for dinner (though having a loose agenda for dinner table conversation isn't a horrible idea!). What it does mean is incorporating relationship priorities and goals into all your long-term planning:

- If you make a bucket list, create three categories: career, relationships, self.

- Plenty of self-help books recommend thinking about your own eulogy. If you do this, picture the various people who might speak. Think about what they'd list as evidence of the close relationships you had with them. Exactly how was your affection for them apparent?

- If you set quarterly goals—which, incidentally, I have found to be a much more effective approach than creating New Year's resolutions—use the same three-category rubric. Each quarter gets a career goal, a relationship goal, and a self goal, giving you twelve major intentions for the calendar year, with the deadlines nicely spread out.

- When you do your Friday planning for the next week, bring all three categories out again. Using a three-category list reminds us that there should be something in all three categories. It's hard to make a three-category list and then leave one of the categories blank!

While career goals are self-explanatory and most people get the idea of personal priorities (such as reading a good book), "relationship priorities" may be puzzling. We don't think of relationship activities as goals, but they can be. Even if they were things we were going to do anyway, consciously identifying them as priorities gives them more mental space, and if the calendar is looking bare, that can be a nudge to reach out to people.

Viewing relationships as their own category of time is transformative in turning these activities from something you do when you have time left over to something that happens. It switches time to kill to time to live right there.

Quality Time amid Quantity Time

The rest of this chapter is about my suggestions for what could go in the relationship category for all those lists of plans and priorities. We often think of relationships as being divided into family, friends, and colleagues, though a more practical way to think of this is that there are people you naturally see multiple times per week and people you don't. These groups will require different sorts of intentionality. One requires creating more meaning within large blocks of time that already exist. The other requires taking steps to have time focused on that other person.

Immediate family members—partners and children—definitely fall into the first category. That's the reality of sharing a home. Even if you're gone from the house sixty hours a week with work obligations and sleeping eight hours a night (fifty-six per week), you would have fifty-two waking hours to account for. If you travel an average of three nights a week, you're home for four. This is a lot of time.

The issue, if you work outside the home, is that many of these hours during the week wind up focused on getting everyone out the door in the morning, and through homework and such in the evening. Weekend hours can easily be consumed by the chores and errands that did not happen during the week. Time does not feel relaxed, especially if you have a brood of little ones, turning kid time into an exercise in crowd control in the best of times, and outright peacekeeping in perilous ones. During one whine-filled October hike, I ran the numbers: if each of my four children is happy 75 percent of the time, and each child's happiness is an independent event, the odds of all four children being happy simultaneously is a mere 31.6 percent.

In other words, even with four generally happy children, two out of three moments will involve an unhappy kid. I love those one-in-three moments when we're all happily splashing in the pool together or enjoying some family fun on a hayride, but I have come to understand that few activities are fun for the whole family for the entire duration. There is transcendence, but there's a lot of muddling involved in getting there.

That's why the best tactic I've found for creating a higher proportion of pleasant, memory-making moments within the hours I spend with my children is to arrange one-on-one time with each of them whenever I can. Many of my immediate family relationship priorities take this exact form: read books to Sam's class, take Jasper to an audition for a show he wanted to do (with no little siblings to distract me). I do a special "Mommy Day" each summer with each child, doing a kid-chosen activity (generally going to an amusement park), and have often wound up doing a solo activity around the child's birthday too. The child looks forward to the special occasion. He or she enjoys the attention. Unhappiness can be nipped in the bud. I get to know the child as an individual, not as part of a team to be managed.

Plenty of other people have found that "monotasking" family

relationships that usually involve a crowd can be transformative. Peter O'Donnell, who runs a consulting firm, undertook a project in 2017 called Grandkids Best Day Ever for his six grandchildren. "Between my wife and I we're creating this summer-long project that picks up on the things these kids have always wanted to do," he explained to me before the summer started. Having a project mind-set automatically nudges things up the priority list, compared with just saying "I'm going to try to attend more of Kason's soccer games." O'Donnell would see his grandkids frequently, but usually in groups or when other things were going on. Planning ahead for solo activities allows for anticipation and the mindfulness that creates deep memories—the sort that seem to stretch time.

So, in addition to attending more of five-year-old Kason's soccer games, O'Donnell and Kason and Kason's parents figured out that he'd really like to go to McDonald's with his grandfather, and teach his grandfather about his favorite video games. Hannah, thirteen, would be going tubing out at the O'Donnell's lake cottage, and going out for a fancy dinner. Kyra, nineteen, would be taking a knife-sharpening class with her grandfather, as part of their plan to cook together. Max, four, would be building a Lego structure or other type of model with O'Donnell, along with stopping at McDonald's, and so forth. "You can wait for opportunities to show up, or you can actually plan them," he says, though of course life doesn't always go as planned. When I checked back in with O'Donnell after the summer was over, I learned that the knife-sharpening class was great, but Max broke his arm, thus putting the Lego building on hold. Kason got really into basketball, so shooting hoops with his grandfather took precedence over the video game tutorial. So it goes—"Even more important than a rigid plan is to make the commitment," he says, and with creative juggling, he spent a lot of special intentional time with these children that might not have happened otherwise.

While special solo days or events are exciting, one-on-one relationship time can be more pedestrian too. People often don't need much. One good relationship goal might be spending a few minutes focused on each family member on the days you're home. Bedtime stories are good for such focus, particularly if you build in enough time to linger if the child wants to chat. Even things that look like inefficiencies can be opportunities. One entrepreneur told me that he and his wife drive their two children to school each morning together. It would make sense to take turns, but doing the school run this way gives them adults-only time in the car together after they drop their kids off. For a few minutes each weekday, they're focused solely on each other—a condition many couples with kids and jobs find to be a rarity.

Of course, going one-on-one isn't the only way to build more meaning into the time people spend with their immediate families. It is really all about intentionality. From studying time logs, I see that even a little thought can do a lot to change something tedious into something more soulful. Few people would show up at work at 8:00 A.M. with no idea about what they'd do until 1:00 P.M., and yet people will come home at 6:00 P.M. having given no thought to what they'll do until they go to bed at 11:00 P.M. This is how people will claim to have no time for their hobbies, even though they're clearly awake for two hours or more after their kids go to bed. It takes effort and thought to pull out a sketchbook, whereas turning on the TV does not. People claim to have no time for their kids or spouses, even if they're all in the house and awake for two to three hours most nights. It is simply that they haven't thought about this time, and so it feels like it doesn't exist.

Setting a relationship intention or two for the evening (or early morning!) allows you to turn this time into something more. It makes this time as important, in your mind, as work—and hence makes it feel more vast. This is true even if what you're doing isn't objectively all that profound. If you and your spouse are doing your taxes, being intentional about it could allow you to build in enough time to discuss your financial (and life) goals. A trip to test-drive new cars could be turned into a date. Maybe you dress up and try a higher-end model, even if you know that's not what you're going to buy. I suspect one reason that meal-kit delivery services have achieved such popularity in the past few years is that they took a pedestrian task (getting dinner on the table) and turned it into an adventurous activity couples could do together. The appetite to deepen time is there; it's simply a matter of putting thought into time that would otherwise slip by.

Why People Want to See You Succeed

Immediate family members have the advantage of physical proximity. In the realm of professional relationships, so do close colleagues. We spend a lot of time at work—not the majority of most people's waking hours, despite the perception, but a lot—and investing in relationships at work can be a great use of time. Feeling close to people you work with means you'll likely produce better work. You'll enjoy it more too. Because work has an unfortunate tendency to produce some clock watching, anything that moves more hours into the pleasant category can transform how we perceive time. It is the difference between feeling dread all Sunday as the hours accelerate into Monday and being genuinely happy when you spend Monday with someone you'd be willing to spend Sunday with too.

Indeed, given that people are people, I believe work relationships are no different from any other relationships. But, as with family members, because we're surrounded by many have-to-dos, it can be easy to relegate relationship building to whatever time is left over. When life is busy, there won't be any time left over, and so the soft side of work gets neglected, or chucked—sometimes self-righteously, based on an underlying notion that it isn't the real substance of a job. I have had people tell me they consider themselves "good" at time management because they don't waste time chatting with colleagues. They shut themselves in their offices, work through lunch, and get stuff done.

This is one approach. It is sometimes done because people

have a hard stop to catch a certain train, or do not wish to take work home. But there are downsides. Being promoted into management, and then managing effectively, isn't just about being able to get the work done. It's about inspiring other people to want to do their best work for you. That is a function of people knowing you and liking you. The only real way to get people to like and trust you is to show you care about their lives, and to spend relaxed, off-the-clock-feeling time with them.

This is true even in professions that don't seem warm and fuzzy. Christopher Brest, whose day job is in law enforcement, has spent the past eighteen years in the army, and these days he's a first sergeant in the reserves. For all the frustrations of military life, "they do a really good job of developing leaders," he says. "It always comes back to people." A good leader learns to build loyalty by never asking anyone to do something he wouldn't do; if Brest's soldiers are digging ditches in the heat, then he's "not going to be sitting in an air-conditioned office drinking coffee." He spends copious quantities of time mentoring future leaders. This "involves a lot of sit-down conversations, closed-door conversations: What are you doing to make yourself better?" He knows when to be gentle. Having been deployed overseas multiple times with very tough, well-trained individuals, he says that "you don't expect people to be sitting on their bunks crying because they're missing their kids, but it happens a lot." He might let a homesick soldier skip out on something to make a phone call. And yes, even in the military, loyalty comes from spending relaxed time together. "The army doesn't necessarily do happy hour," he says, "but we might play football during [physical training] time instead of doing push-ups." A leader who throws in a bit of levity and shows he cares about people produces what cartoonish drill sergeant–yelling cannot: soldiers who trust their leader enough to do whatever he asks.

So it is with leadership in the civilian world too. Indeed, if you rise up through the ranks, all those in-the-hall chats and lunches and happy hours that seem like they're not real work can become a critical part of your job. Andrew Glincher, the CEO and managing partner of law firm Nixon Peabody, whom we met in chapter 4, makes a point of going to any reception or casual get-together being held at an office he's visiting. "It's an opportunity to spend time with many more people," he explains. "Any gathering of people can be a very valuable use of time." There can be big wins: solving someone's minor problem before it festers might keep her from quitting, and taking a major client with her to a competitor.

Even if you have no intention of ever moving out of an individual contributor role, professional success still stems from solid relationships. Other people might have insights into office politics, or might have ideas you haven't contemplated, or might have made stupid mistakes they can warn you about. Gleaning this information in the company cafeteria can be a more efficient use of your lunch break than eating at your desk.

Because you do see your colleagues frequently, it's relatively easy to build relaxed time into your work life. This doesn't have to become the either/or matter that people often convince themselves it is when it comes to work/life balance. People stuck in what I call the "24-hour trap" think, *If I go to happy hour with my colleagues I won't see my kids!* Perhaps you won't that one night, but the week is vast. Going out or staying a little later one or two nights per week means you're home the other five or six, which hardly sounds imbalanced. So if people go out for drinks after work, go sometimes. Not every night (does anyone go every night?), but if you say yes sometimes, then people will still ask. If the answer is always no, they know there's no point.

There are plenty of opportunities during the workday too. If you've got a one-on-one meeting with someone, suggest moving it to a coffee shop or going for a walk. Changing venues changes mind-sets, and that can allow for genuine engagement.

As you set your weekly professional priorities, include a lunch or breakfast with someone you want to get to know. Even normal conversations can be had mindfully. Observing good conversationalists, I see that they ask questions that let the other person tell his or her favorite stories. When they ask about someone's weekend, they listen to the answer. They don't try to top the story, and if they redirect things, they're careful to phrase the redirection in a way that makes it clear they understand the other person's priorities.

The realization: everyone—*everyone*—likes to feel heard. In his law enforcement work, Brest has found that "as a general rule, people care about themselves and how it's going to benefit them." If he's interrogating a suspect in a jail cell, that person could not care less about Brest's progress in the case. He's only going to share information if it's personally helpful to him. So that's how the conversation must be shaped. One study of the most effective meetings found they included a few dedicated minutes at the start for chitchat, with everyone getting a chance to say what was important to him or her. Giving such chitchat a spot on the agenda gave it a time limit (so no one snarls, "We don't have time for this!"), but having it happen meant that team members felt comfortable with one another. When teams feel close, their work tends to be more creative and efficient. Much time can be wasted on jockeying for attention or figuring out if a person was making a veiled insult, and on other things that don't happen when people interact with an assumption of trust. Trust takes time, but people are a good use of time. It's worth building in.

Reach Out

Colleagues and family members fall into the category of people you see frequently. People outside your organization—or even in different parts of your organization—fall into that second category: relationships involving people you don't naturally see frequently. The human brain often has trouble focusing on such people, which makes sense. If our cave-dwelling ancestors didn't see someone for a while, it was probably because the person was dead, not because he was telecommuting.

But such relationships are still worth putting on the priority list, which brings me to the topic of "networking." If I could, I would chuck this word and its transactional connotation entirely. Understood well, networking is nothing more than building authentic relationships with people whom you want to see succeed and who feel the same way about you. Some people go overboard on so-called networking in an obnoxious way. No one likes that guy at a conference who's constantly looking over people's shoulders to find someone more important to talk to. But in my experience, the more frequent networking sin is underdoing it. People aren't actively looking for new jobs, so they don't bother meeting people outside their organizations. That's fine, except few jobs are permanent these days. Job security is best defined as having a handful of people who've told you, "If you ever think of switching jobs, come talk to me first." That happens only when people get to know you and decide they like you.

The good news is that nurturing a thriving network doesn't take nearly as much face-to-face engagement as you might think. As a free agent, work-from-home sort, I am often pleasantly surprised by this. There are people I've seen in person half a dozen times, total, over five years, whom I would call my friends and who I believe would say the same of me. The key is supplementing occasional meetings with all the other ways of communicating. Indeed, it's about making such communication a habit.

The best advice I've heard on this—strengthening a network

among people you don't see frequently—is to reach out to one person every day.

Molly Beck, author of the book *Reach Out,* calls this the "RO" habit. Every Friday while you're planning your week, make a list of five people you'd like to reach out to. These can be:

- "Re-ROs," who are people you've met in the past and wish to keep in touch with.

- "Follow-up ROs," who are people you met recently at events and want to establish ties with.

- "Borrowed Connection ROs," who are people your friends and colleagues think you should meet.

- "Cool ROs," who are people you don't know but think are interesting.

Be judicious in the last category; spamming famous people doesn't do much for you or them. But if you liked a book you read or were impressed by someone quoted in an article or interviewed on TV, the person would like to hear that. These emails do tend to get read, even if they don't always garner responses.

You can draft notes to these five people at once (think eight to ten minutes apiece) or do one each morning. Start with a compliment, and offer something helpful, like a recommendation. If you ask for advice, make sure you can't Google the answer. These emails can be simple. I was the target of a Beck RO in 2013, when she found my email address and wrote to thank me for retweeting a link to her blog (where she had written about one of my books). The entire note was 110 words long, but it did the job. I have been attentively following her career ever since.

Unlike the normal vision of networking, doing a daily RO "doesn't take much time," says Beck. "You don't have to find childcare." You don't have to live near a major city. "If you have an internet connection, you can start doing this tomorrow." If you send 250 emails a year, and hear back from 40 percent of these people, that's a hundred responses. If you talk with or meet twenty of these people, those are a lot of solid connections right there. "You have to make it a process for whatever you want to do," says Beck. Indeed, she used the same approach for meeting her husband. She (and he!) were both systematic about online dating, going on at least one first date each week. Eventually they met each other, and the other first dates stopped.

I'm sure champion networkers are clucking about such a limited goal: *Just one person per day?* They've graduated from reaching out daily to introducing people in their networks to each other daily, which is a beautiful skill if you have it. I do not. Different brains work in different ways. I am unlikely to think, *Oh, I know Beth, and she likes French art, and so does Mary. Mary will be visiting Boston, which is where Beth lives. I should suggest they get together.* Those of us without intuitive connecting skills have to do what we can, knowing that something is better than nothing.

As it is, the something might be better than we think it is. I was lamenting on my blog that I wasn't reaching out or networking as often as I should, when someone pointed out that for the past fifteen years I've been writing at least one article a week for various publications. This generally involves interviewing at least two people. So I was reaching out to at least one hundred people a year in a professional context, both experts and "real people," and I was getting to know them, and following up with them, and writing about them again, and talking about people's books and projects. That is networking. It just didn't look like me hustling at a cocktail hour.

Speaking of which, I believe that the one-person-a-day habit is the best antidote to networking event nerves and the ensuing overreach. You feel no pressure to collect ten business cards. You know you'll be reaching out to ten people over the next ten days anyway, so you can relax. You can go in desiring nothing but interesting conversations with interesting people. That might be defined as interesting professionally, or it could mean getting a good restaurant or book recommendation. Those can be a source of pleasure too.

How to Make Time for Friends

As with professional contacts who don't work in the same office, friends often fall into the category of people you don't naturally see multiple times per week. My articles on making time for friends have been among my most shared, and I think it's because these are the relationships that are most likely to fall apart during the busy years. Work gets done because the mortgage needs to be paid. Even if you and your spouse only see each other over piles of laundry, that sheer frequency can keep things humming along. Setting aside time for friends, on the other hand, can feel incredibly self-indulgent. If you're telling yourself the story that you work long hours and hence never see your kids, you may believe you can't take two hours on a Saturday to meet a friend for a long run, or spend a weekend visiting a friend in Boise. But unless you're the guy who's sitting at the pub with his mates for three hours after work daily, I'm guessing you could spare more friend time in your life. Good friends energize you, which makes it possible to handle work and family responsibilities.

There are several ways to make friendships a priority in your life, and to make sure the category of relationship goals includes friends alongside the people you're related to and work with.

First, go big. Oddly enough, big events can be easier to prioritize than small ones. Even if you're busy, you'll likely go to a good friend's wedding, so if you'd like to see far-flung friends, become the instigator of a similarly grand occasion. Give people the date for a long weekend get-together a year in advance. Book somewhere fabulous. Invite their significant others and children. This keeps them from feeling guilty for leaving everyone, and when people's families become friends, it tightens ties with a second layer of bonding. As everyone is reveling in the first weekend, enjoying off-the-clock time over wine while the kids are in bed, book the date for a second get-together. Eventually, your annual weekend will take on a life of its own.

Another option: make standing dates for smaller get-togethers with local friends. One-off events can be fun, but they may take more work to plan than seems worthwhile for a single evening. People are busy, and the more people you try to get together, the bigger the logistical challenge. Recurring events, however, feature none of these woes. If you know your book club gets together on the first Thursday night of the month, no one needs to think about it. Your friends know to hold the date open unless an emergency comes up. Their families (and colleagues!) know to plan for this time. A bonus of any regular get-together: you'll start looking forward to those first Thursday nights. You'll know that even if you haven't done much with friends lately, you'll see your friends the next Thursday, which reminds you that you are the kind of person who has friends.

One-on-one friend coordination is obviously easier, but these relationships still benefit from having a regular spot on the calendar. Cathy Doggett and Elisabeth McKetta usually speak each Monday. If their call doesn't happen Monday, they know to try again on Tuesday. Meeting a friend for breakfast every Friday morning turns time with him from something you'd like to have happen to something that most likely does happen.

If recurring get-togethers aren't going to work, the next best option is to align your time. This is multitasking in a nice way.

You take something you need or want to do, and incorporate a friend into it as well. As I think about it, this is how much of my friend time happens at this stage in my life. I have a few running buddies whom I chat with to pass the miles; you could sign up for an exercise class with someone you want to see more often. Taking on a regular volunteering gig with a friend means you'll see each other at board meetings. Commuting offers alignment opportunities; you might take the same bus to work together sometimes, or carpool, even if it's slightly less convenient. I have met up with friends on business trips to New York, San Diego, Seattle, Nashville. My podcast is the ultimate in alignment. Sarah and I took something fun that we didn't do all that often—chat with each other about our lives and careers—and turned it into something our audience now expects us to do frequently. Convincing a friend to join you in a side hustle or in managing a professional organization pretty much guarantees you will see each other more often. It will definitely make your work more fun.

Be Choosy

Finally—and this brings us to the magic of Doggett and McKetta's friendship—making relationships a priority means being selective about the people with whom you choose to spend your hours. For various reasons, some people have more people in their lives than others. Some people live near a large extended family. Some people have a family member who's prominent in a community. Some people are more extroverted than others, and some have collected people into their lives through past associations (such as a fraternity or a college sports team). While people are a good use of time, time is still ultimately limited, and so the hard truth for these people whose lives are people-focused is that not all relationships are going to last through the years when you are building a career, or raising a family, or doing both. Not all relationships will last through moves or career changes. Some winnowing is natural as you discover which people you were close to because they truly deepen your spirit and which people you were close to because it was convenient.

You may also discover along the way that some people are never going to deepen your spirit. Most friendships (and family relationships, for that matter) get better with work, but sometimes the work required is more than seems worthwhile. That's OK. The goal is quality, not quantity. The goal is figuring out which relationships are worth investing in even if they are not convenient. And then the goal is to go all in on making these relationships work.

This requires conscious choices about how to spend time. Despite the song's instruction to "make new friends but keep the old," when time is limited, these activities can be at odds. You can invite a new friend to coffee, or you can renew ties with an older friend by doing the same thing. If the old friend doesn't live nearby, you can spend that same time talking on the phone. McKetta reports that Doggett has a handful of other friends like her that she has kept for a very long time. "She gardens them," she says. It's easy to spend time on the people right around you whom you see frequently. Consciously devoting limited time to people who aren't right around you "requires incredible discipline," says McKetta. "It's like working on a book as opposed to answering email: you have to plan for it and inconvenience yourself to plan for it."

This mind-set can be somewhat enigmatic for the people who *are* around you frequently. You might risk seeming unfriendly. I know I struggled with some people initially seeming this way when I moved from New York City, where transience is understood, to my community in Pennsylvania, where it is not. Indeed, many people grew up here. They have deep ties to friends and family that we could not easily become a part of. As one parent who was also new in the area joked to me on the playground, the message was, "We made our friends in fifth grade. We don't need any more friends!" This mind-set sounds insular to outsiders, but for these tight-knit groups, it is a recipe for human happiness to still be surrounded, in midlife, by the friends you made as a child. These people know you beyond the trappings of whom you married, what you do for a living, and whether your children are star students or total screwups. Introducing new people into the dynamic might upset it, and might be more of a risk than people are willing to take.

Fortunately, in any community, there are always those who are willing to include newcomers in their lives, and there are other newcomers too, and you can all support one another as you figure out your place in the world. And, of course, you can invest in older relationships as well, going back to visit people, carving out time to talk, and going all in on what makes relationships work. We might understand that romantic relationships require discussing the relationship and issues we might have, but we don't necessarily think of this with friendships. "I'd really never talked about a friendship with a friend," says McKetta of life before Doggett. But "Cathy and I have talked about it. She will put it in the room. She will say, 'This thing didn't work for me. Can we talk about it?' She always gets directly to the thing, so we can return to a place of peace and lightness and ease."

And if something does not return to peace, lightness, and ease? The hard truth about caring for other people is that any relationship can end. Viewed from a certain perspective they all will end, at least in this world. But alongside that depressing thought, there is this positive one: all that we love becomes a part of us. Whatever happiness we had is still there in memory, and memories can be polished like jewels instead of locked up in drawers. The happiness of the memory does not hinge on the present. I love this line in Wendell Berry's book *Jayber Crow*: "It is not a terrible thing to love the world, knowing that the world is always passing and irrecoverable, to be known only in loss. To love anything good, at any cost, is a bargain."

Holding back as a hedge against pain is pointless, as pain is inevitable. Wisdom is accepting the reality of pain and loving anyway. And if you are loving anyway, you may as well let people know it. That is part of recognizing that people are a good use of time.

I'm not a gushy person, so to me it feels most authentic to think and talk about specific ways people add to my life. Many of my "reach out" emails are simply thank-you notes: to my kids' teachers for something they learned, to people who've written things that make me think, to a friend for asking me over to drink wine in her kitchen on a Wednesday afternoon when I really needed to escape from my office. Even in the midst of the most demanding years, there can be much to be grateful for. Here is what all the people in my life—which very much includes the four little people in my life—have done for me: I have a more profound sense of time's value, and memories that are both more ridiculous and poignant than I ever would have had otherwise.

Amazement Through Someone Else's Eyes

I try to take the memory-making opportunities that have presented themselves during the circus of these past few years. When I remember that "people are a good use of time," I start thinking about ways to create memories with the people I care about. I think about what I would like to see typed on my time logs someday far in the future, when I look back and study my time.

It was this desire for experiences that led me to suggest Jasper's Christmas present for the year he was nine. He desperately wanted a cat or a dog. He did not get one, because I did not think I could care for yet another living thing. We discussed our options, and he agreed that I could take him on a two-night visit to New York City instead when he had some days off school in February. I gave him a guidebook and told him to choose our activities. He picked out the most touristy ones, which makes sense, I suppose. He was unlikely to insist on an off-the-radar jazz club or some too-hip-for-reservations vegan brunch spot. So, swallowing my pride, I bought tickets for the top of the Empire State Building, the ferry to the Statue of Liberty, and *The Lion King* on Broadway. We also planned to see the Central Park Zoo.

Travel with a nine-year-old is easier than travel with a two-year-old, but still, it's a kid. New York has amazing restaurants, and we couldn't eat at any of them. Even pizza was problematic, because some places make only gourmet-style pizzas with splotches of mozzarella and giant basil leaves, and my son prefers the sort of uniform pizza cheese that comes in the DiGiorno box. I was grateful to find an Au Bon Pain with mac 'n' cheese as one of their soup flavors, and a pub that—catering to parents hauling their children around the theater district—advertised its kid menu. Craft beer for me, hot chocolate and chicken tenders for him.

And yet, it was still such a wonderful experience. We watched the sun set from the 102nd floor of the Empire State Building, the sky glowing pink over the Hudson and the East River. The next day we gawked at the city from the ferry, and Central Park even on a wintry afternoon was magical. In the zoo, the snow leopard padded within feet of us. The red panda—who normally sleeps the vast majority of the day—scooted around the trees. My son asked about taking a carriage ride, and because it was something I had always wanted to do but could not justify for just my frugal self, I said yes. We snuggled up under the covers. We circled Central Park like we would have in Frederick Law Olmsted's day. Our driver told us that our horse needed to stretch her legs, and so we flew beneath the bare trees and skyscrapers. I couldn't stop smiling, nor could Jasper, because he knew that, even after this fun, we still had *Lion King* tickets for that night.

We snuggled on one of the hotel beds later, and talked about our day. I know in a few years such things will be in our past. Jasper is already nearly as tall as I am. But for now he is just an eager little kid. He is still excited to go on a boat, a subway, a taxi, an elevator. Having lived in Manhattan for years, I am jaded about so many New York things, but I remember moving there at age twenty-three and being so in awe of it myself. I was so in awe of little things like blue flowers in the delis on the corner, there at any hour for the buying. White flowers I could see. But blue!

For two days I experienced this amazement through someone else's eyes. I will never be that twenty-three-year-old girl again, partly because of the existence of my son and all his siblings. But being with this child brought some of that joy back, a joy I don't think could be accessed in any other way. It came solely by loving this person, and sharing the gift of time.

July again. One year since that morning in Maine. It was another perfect summer day: warm, but not heavily so, the blue sky marbled by wisps of clouds. I was on my bike twenty miles northwest of Philadelphia, and again in a situation with no immediate claims on my time. I had booked a sitter to take care of Alex so that my husband and I could take the three older kids to a pool party in New Jersey. Then we learned some of the kids' good friends planned to come to the party earlier in the day. So my husband took off with the older kids several hours before we originally planned to leave, leaving me with Alex until the sitter could get there, at which point I figured they didn't really need me in New Jersey. I was free to do what I wished.

I put my bike in my car and drove to the Valley Forge trailhead. No one would expect me back until much later than I had any intention (or capability) of biking, so I didn't need to look at the time. The path was smooth enough that I could let my mind roam.

Alas, it kept wandering to life logistics. Again and again and again.

It makes sense. It's tough to turn everything off, and it had been a rough week. I had given three speeches in three states in thirty hours. I had taken two kids to see specialists about things. The next week would bring more travel, and the pressing question of whether I needed another driver to deal with an extra round of swim lessons I'd just signed two kids up for. And yet, I wasn't going to be able to do anything about any of that from my bike. I had arranged those open hours to pedal twenty miles on the Schuylkill River Trail. Why couldn't I just enjoy them?

In the past few years, I have done much to become more aware of the hours whose existence I have faithfully logged. I have built adventures into my days, and cleared my schedule of much that I don't want in the remaining 400,000 (or so) hours of my life. I was investing in my happiness in that moment, having kept the sitter despite my absence from the pool party. I was then trying to linger in those moments along the trail, stretching the experience of feeling no obligation. But there is always a space between knowing and doing. Some days I leap it as easily as I do the rocks in the stream on a favorite running route. Other days, it is a chasm.

I hear this from people all the time. *I know what I should do, I just don't.* Perhaps you feel this way having read this book. You took notes on things you'd like to try, but what turns desires into Monday-morning reality?

There is no easy answer to this, other than to know that using time better is a process. No one ever parks her bike at the ultimate trailhead. Instead you should aim to do just one small thing better today, and then take another step the next day. Rather than lament all that doesn't work, become aware of that one small step. Often, it can be the moment that becomes the reality of that day in memory.

That was the case for me along that trail. Somewhere amid my mental patter, I emerged from the woods to a clearing where the river flowed right there beside me. My mind jarred to a stop. I breathed in the wildflowers and all this slow water's magnificence. For a moment, I could think of nothing except the wind on my face, the sun on my arms, the birds cawing overhead. *Beautiful, beautiful,* I felt the words swimming around my brain.

That is the image I will remember when I think about that bike ride, not the mental clutter. That sudden sense of freedom can crowd out all else, at least for a bit. All time passes. But some moments transcend the ceaseless ticking. We simply need to see them, and then in time, we see more.

Feeling less busy while getting more done is a process. The next few pages have exercises and questions to help you analyze your time, so you can spend it better, and feel better about how you spend it too.

Track Your Time

If you'd like to spend your time better, the first step is figuring out where it goes now. Following is the time log I use to track my weeks; you can fill out the subscription form to be emailed an Excel or PDF copy at LauraVanderkam.com.

Write down what you're doing a few times per day. Broad categories are OK: work, sleep, hang out with spouse, drive, grocery shopping, et cetera. The point is to have a holistic picture

	MONDAY	TUESDAY	WEDNESDAY
5 A.M.			
5:30			
6			
6:30			
7			
7:30			
8			
8:30			
9			
9:30			
10			
10:30			
11			
11:30			
12 P.M.			
12:30			
1			
1:30			
2			
2:30			
3			
3:30			
4			
4:30			

URSDAY	FRIDAY	SATURDAY	SUNDAY

(cont. on next page)

(cont. from previous page)

	MONDAY	TUESDAY	WEDNESDAY
5 P.M.			
5:30			
6			
6:30			
7			
7:30			
8			
8:30			
9			
9:30			
10			
10:30			
11			
11:30			
12 A.M.			
12:30			
1			
1:30			
2			
2:30			
3			
3:30			
4			
4:30			

HURSDAY	FRIDAY	SATURDAY	SUNDAY

of your time, not to document every minute. If there's a category of time you're concerned about (or proud of!) you can track that more closely. Recording a whole week is best, but even a few days can be helpful. Try two workdays and one weekend day. Remember: there are no typical weeks!

Tend Your Garden

After tracking your time, look back over your schedule and ask yourself a few questions:

What do I like about my schedule?
What would I like to spend more time doing?
What would I like to spend less time doing?
How can I make that happen?

Thinking through your days and weeks before you're in them increases the chances that this time is spent on meaningful and enjoyable things.

Picture a "realistic ideal day." Within the parameters of your current responsibilities, what would a realistic ideal day look like? How about a realistic ideal week?

On Friday afternoons, look at the week ahead. Make yourself a three-category priority list: career, relationships, self. Which two or three items should go in each category? Look at the upcoming week. Where can these things go?

Create daily intentions. If you did nothing else today, what three accomplishments would make you feel like you got a lot done?

Make Life Memorable

Why will today be different from other days? Why will tomorrow be different from other days?

Make a list of adventures you'd like to have over the course of your life. These can be big (travel to Paris) or small (try that new restaurant that just opened across the street). You're not committing to any of these, so list anything that comes to mind as a possibility. Revisit this list several times over the next few days, and see what you can add to it. If you brainstorm a lot of related adventures, consider making a project for yourself (for example, visiting all the national parks in California).

Carve out time for evoking memories. Look at an old photo album. Listen to music that was important to you during a certain period of your life. Stop by a place that was formative for you. Write down the memories that bubble up, or share them with someone else. How does this change how you feel about time?

Don't Fill Time

Look at the activities and commitments that currently fill your life. If you were starting from a blank slate, which of these would you add now?

For everything else, is there a way you can wind these down

over the next few months? If you can't extricate yourself from these commitments, how can you minimize the time devoted to them?

What activities do you do frequently? How can you streamline the logistical aspects of these activities to open up space?

Celebrate your time dividends. Look at your life and see which things you're doing now that take much less time than they have in the past, or could have taken more time if you'd made different choices. Make a note of these (and refer to them anytime you feel less than productive).

Put the phone in airplane mode. Challenge yourself to keep it in airplane mode for longer stretches of time. Pay special attention to little bits of time during the day when you're waiting, and the time before bed on weekdays. If you avoid social media, what could you do with this time instead?

Linger

Look at your calendar for anything coming up that you know will be pleasurable (such as a beach vacation where you'll have a great view of the sunset, or a long-anticipated dinner with an old friend). Think ahead of time about strategies you might use to savor and stretch the moment. Can you express to others how much you're enjoying yourself? Can you make a mental note about details: sights, sounds, smells? Can you try to be as alert as possible? Can you remind yourself how long you've waited for it? Can you picture yourself in the future, describing this scene to someone else?

To increase your enjoyment of normal life, try creating a constructed contrast. Can you picture some darker moment in the future when you will miss your current daily activities? Let your mind go there, briefly. Then open your eyes. Does this make you feel differently about your routine tasks?

Try creating a mini daily vacation. Can you build a few minutes into your life today to consciously savor something? It could be smelling a flower on the walk to work, or reading a really good book on the subway, or looking at a photo on your desk and savoring the memory of that time. Challenge yourself to max out your enjoyment. What do you do to maximize the pleasure?

Invest in Your Happiness

Look at your time log and figure out particular pain points in your life. When are you counting the minutes? What could you do to move minutes out of this category?

What are your favorite treats? Could you put these into your life more frequently?

Which activities make you happiest? Could you plan these into your schedule first, either by blocking them into mornings or by scheduling them for the beginning of the week?

Let It Go

Notice which topics take up a lot of mental space. What do you keep thinking about? What role do your self-imposed expectations play in this rumination?

For which low-stakes matters in your life could you lower your standards?

What good habits do you want to build? How low would you have to lower your expectations to feel no resistance to doing that habit daily? For example, someone wanting to exercise might decide to do ten minutes per day. Someone wanting to write a novel might commit to writing two hundred words per day.

What would it mean to be gentle with yourself?

People Are a Good Use of Time

Which relationships would you like to invest more time in?

What activities would enhance the time you spend with people you're close to?

A thriving network can be built over time by reaching out to one person daily. Which five people would you like to connect with this week?

ACKNOWLEDGMENTS

I am grateful to everyone who helped make this book possible.

Thanks to Leah Trouwborst and the team at Portfolio for shepherding yet another book from idea to finished product, and to Emilie Stewart of the Emilie Stewart Literary Agency for representing my projects.

Thanks to Ardyn Nordstrom for her assistance designing and analyzing the time-diary study on which *Off the Clock* is based. I am particularly grateful to all the busy people who took time out of their lives to complete the survey, and to everyone who was willing to share their stories and the details of their schedules.

Thanks to Nancy Sheed and the team at Sheed Communications for all their help with marketing this book and my previous ones.

Thanks to Sarah Hart-Unger for devoting many hours to launching and cohosting the *Best of Both Worlds* podcast, and to Phyllis Nichols of Sound Advice Sales & Marketing for producing it.

Thanks to Katherine Reynolds Lewis for holding me accountable to my ideas for the past few years.

Thanks to my blog readers and the audience members at my speeches, who have provided valuable feedback on what time-management strategies work in real life.

As I work to manage my own time, I'm grateful to Gabrielle, Jess, my parents, and my mother-in-law for their help with the kids and home life in general. And thanks to Michael, Jasper, Sam, Ruth, and Alex for making all my hours more meaningful.

INTRODUCTION: THE TIME PARADOX

5 **Gallup conducts frequent polls on time stress:** Frank Newport, "Americans' Perceived Time Crunch No Worse Than in Past," *Gallup News*, December 31, 2015, http://news.gallup.com/poll/187982/americans-perceived-time-crunch-no-worse-past.aspx.

8 **a phenomenon that supports other time-diary study findings:** For one analysis of systematic biases in time estimation, compared with studies looking at "yesterday," see John P. Robinson and Geoffrey Godbey, *Time for Life: The Surprising Ways Americans Use Their Time* (University Park, PA: The Pennsylvania State University Press, 1997).

10 **On April 15, 2017, an Italian woman named Emma Morano:** "Ancient as the hills," *The Economist*, April 29, 2017, 74.

10 **Tables from the Centers for Disease Control reveal:** *Health, United States, 2016*, a publication of the U.S. Department of Health and Human Services. For an approximation of my at-65 life expectancy (using 1980), see table 15: www.cdc.gov/nchs/data/hus/hus16.pdf#015.

14 **In one of the most famous experiments in social science:** E. J. Langer and J. Rodin, "The Effects of Choice and Enhanced Personal Responsibility for the Aged: A Field Experiment in an Institutional Setting," *Journal of Personality and Social Psychology* 34, no. 2 (August 1976): 191–98, www.ncbi.nlm.nih.gov/pub med/1011073.

CHAPTER 1: TEND YOUR GARDEN

25 **As famed landscape architect Beatrix Farrand once said:** "New York Society Girl a Landscape Architect," *New York Daily Tribune*, February 11, 1900, as cited in *Beatrix Jones Farrand: Fifty Years of American Landscape Architecture* (Washington, D.C.: Dumbarton Oaks, Trustees for Harvard University, 1982).

31 **I love to highlight a study finding that people claiming 75-plus-hour workweeks:** John P. Robinson et al., "The Overestimated Workweek Revisited," *Monthly Labor Review* (Bureau of Labor Statistics), June 2011, www.bls.gov/opub/mlr/2011/06/art3full.pdf.

32 **the American Time Use Survey pegs this at about eighteen hours per week:** American Time Use Survey, Table 8B, "Time Spent in Primary Activities for the Civilian Population 18 Years and Over by Presence and Age of Youngest Household Child and Sex, 2016 Annual Averages, Employed," Bureau of Labor Statistics, www.bls.gov/news .release/atus.t08b.htm. For employed women with at least one child under the age of six, the daily average is 1.93 hours on "household activities" and 0.73 hours on "purchasing goods and services." Adding and multiplying for a seven-day week gives us 18.62 hours.

47 **More than three hundred Parks Department employees:** Figures are from the Central Park Conservancy website's "Park History," www .centralparknyc.org/visit/park-history.html.

50 **Rowling spouted this little gem:** Heather Hogan, "JK Rowling Tells Oprah: 'Harry Is Still in My Head. I Could Definitely Write an Eighth, a Ninth Book,' October 1, 2010, AfterEllen.com, www.afterellen.com /people/79725-jk-rowling-tells-oprah-harry-is-still-in-my-head-i-could -definitely-write-an-eighth-a-ninth-book.

CHAPTER 2: MAKE LIFE MEMORABLE

57 **"we want more time," said NYU psychology professor Lila Davachi:** Davachi's TED Talk is available at www.youtube.com/watch?v=

zUqs3y9ucaU. Quotes are from both the talk and an interview with Davachi.

60 **As philosopher and psychologist William James writes on time:** All quotes from William James, *The Principles of Psychology, Volume 1* (New York: Dover Publications, Inc., 1950 [first published by Henry Holt and Company, 1890]).

72 **Writes philosopher Robert Grudin:** All quotes are from Robert Grudin, *Time and the Art of Living* (New York: Harper & Row, 1981).

76 **Research supports this poetic notion:** Joseph E. Dunsmoor et al., "Emotional Learning Selectively and Retroactively Strengthens Memories for Related Events," *Nature* 520 (April 16, 2015): 345–48, www.nature.com /nature/journal/v520/n7547/abs/nature14106.html?foxtrotcallback=true.

CHAPTER 3: DON'T FILL TIME

83 **"Curious, he phoned the assistant to this special manager":** Ken Blanchard, PhD, and Spencer Johnson, MD, *The New One Minute Manager* (New York: William Morrow, 2015).

86 **Edith Wharton, that shrewd observer of humanity:** All quotes from Edith Wharton, *Twilight Sleep* (originally published 1927, many editions currently available).

91 **Don't just chuck stuff you don't like:** Marie Kondo, *The Life-Changing Magic of Tidying Up: The Japanese Art of Decluttering and Organizing* (Berkeley, CA: Ten Speed Press, 2014), 41.

109 **the average social media consumer spends 116 minutes per day on these sites:** Mediakix, "How Much Time Do We Spend on Social Media?" http://mediakix.com/2016/12/how-much-time-is-spent-on-social -media-lifetime/#gs.=JFYHY4.

109 **For a study published in *Computers in Human Behavior* in 2015:** Kostadin Kushlev and Elizabeth W. Dunn, "Checking Email Less Frequently Reduces Stress," *Computers in Human Behavior* 43 (February 2015): 220–28.

113   **This is the spirit of that Mary Oliver poem:** Mary Oliver, "The Summer Day," *The House of Light* (Boston: Beacon Press, 1990).

CHAPTER 4: LINGER

120   **So are many people who fall into the "upholder" category:** Gretchen Rubin, *The Four Tendencies: The Indispensable Personality Profiles That Reveal How to Make Your Life Better (and Other People's Lives Better, Too)* (New York: Harmony, 2017).

122   **In one famous experiment, seminary students:** John M. Darley and C. Daniel Batson, "'From Jerusalem to Jericho': A Study of Situational and Dispositional Variables in Helping Behavior," *Journal of Personality and Social Psychology* 27, no. 1 (1973): 100–108.

126   **You become like Mrs. Ramsay in *To The Lighthouse*:** Virginia Woolf, *To the Lighthouse* (New York: Harcourt Brace and Company, 1927), 111.

128   **In their 2006 book *Savoring*:** See Appendix D of Fred B. Bryant and Joseph Veroff, *Savoring: A New Model of Positive Experience* (Mahwah, NJ: Lawrence Erlbaum Associates, 2007).

128   **For what is essentially a research:** Ibid.

136   **In 2017's *The Little Book of Hygge*:** Meik Wiking, *The Little Book of Hygge: Danish Secrets to Happy Living* (New York: William Morrow, 2017).

CHAPTER 5: INVEST IN YOUR HAPPINESS

144   **Studies of human happiness find:** For one discussion of subjective well-being, see Daniel Kahneman and Alan B. Krueger, "Developments in the Measurement of Subjective Well-being," *Journal of Economic Perspectives* 20, no. 1 (Winter 2006): 3–24, http://pubs.aeaweb.org/doi/pdfplus/10.1257/089533006776526030.

159   **That's the case for Amelia Boone:** For a list of Amelia Boone's awards, see www.ameliabooneracing.com/raceschedule.html.

CHAPTER 6: LET IT GO

173 **from the *Dhammapada*:** Thomas Byrom, "Desire," *The Dhamma-pada: The Sayings of the Buddha* (New York: Vintage, 2012), https://books.google.com/books?isbn=0307950719.

176 **Schwartz told me when I interviewed him:** Laura Vanderkam, "The Surprising Scientific Link Between Happiness and Decision-Making," *Fast Company*, August 23, 2016, www.fastcompany.com/3063066/the-science-backed-way-to-be-happier-by-making-better-choices.

176 **"Of the seven deadly sins":** Joseph Epstein, *Envy*, The Seven Deadly Sins (New York: Oxford University Press, 2003), 1.

177 **As philosopher (and novelist) Alain de Botton:** Alain de Botton, "Why You Will Marry the Wrong Person," *New York Times*, May 28, 2016, www.nytimes.com/2016/05/29/opinion/sunday/why-you-will-marry-the-wrong-person.html.

182 **people who do something daily for decades:** For my original write-up of my father's Hebrew reading streak, please see Laura Vanderkam, "The Secrets of People Who Manage to Stick to Habit Changes," *Fast Company*, July 12, 2016, www.fastcompany.com/3061665/the-secrets-of-people-who-manage-to-stick-to-habit-changes.

189 **"Do not worry":** Ernest Hemingway, *A Moveable Feast* (New York: Scribner, 1964), 12.

CHAPTER 7: PEOPLE ARE A GOOD USE OF TIME

191 **phone interview with Elisabeth McKetta and Cathy Doggett:** Please see Laura Vanderkam, "How to Be a Better Friend, Even When You're Busy," *Fast Company*, www.fastcompany.com/3057746/how-to-be-a-better-friend-even-when-youre-busy.

193 **"Let there be no purpose in friendship save the deepening of the spirit":** All quotes from Kahlil Gibran, *The Prophet* (New York: Alfred A. Knopf, 1923).

196 **People with tight social ties tend to live longer:** A number of studies have looked at this phenomenon. For a summary of such research, please see Katherine Harmon, "Social Ties Boost Survival by 50 Percent," *Scientific American,* July 28, 2010, www.scientificamerican.com/article/relationships-boost-survival.

209 **One study of the most effective meetings:** Please see Kathryn Parker Boudett and Elizabeth A. City, *Meeting Wise: Making the Most of Collaborative Time for Educators* (Cambridge, MA: Harvard Education Press, 2014).

211 **Molly Beck, author of the book *Reach Out:*** Molly Beck, *Reach Out: The Simple Strategy You Need to Expand Your Network and Increase Your Influence* (New York: McGraw-Hill, 2017).

219 **I love this line in Wendell Berry's book *Jayber Crow*:** Wendell Berry, *Jayber Crow* (Berkeley, CA: Counterpoint, 2000), 329.